That Close: a memory of combat in Vietnam
Robert Driskill

Table of Contents

Prologue

April 1969

Chapter One

An Education

Chapter Two

Basic Training

Chapter Three

Lieutenant Pace

The booby trap

Chapter Four

The Jungle

Chapter Five

Thanksgiving

Chapter Six

Walter Reed

Chapter Seven

That Close

Chapter Eight

Don't Mean Nothin'

Prologue

April 1969

In the early evening of April 17, 1969, the six available members of Sergeant Bull's squad filed out of Fire Base Chris, a sandbag-walled compound about ten miles southwest of Saigon. They were one of three squads that made up Third Platoon, Charley Company, Fifth Battalion of the Twelfth Regiment, 199th Light Infantry Brigade. Charley Company made its home in Chris, nightly sending out patrols like the one Sergeant Bull was leading. At the time, the 199th was tasked with "securing the southern and western approaches to Saigon." This area was part of the Mekong Delta, a vast waterlogged area of rice paddies and small fishing and farming villages, laced with rivers and canals and dotted with small patches of Nipa Palm jungle.

Some of the minor details of the patrol -- who was where in line, who had the radio-telephone -- are unknown to me. But probably Larry Lauzon, a married twenty-four-year-old native of West Virginia, walked point. He had only been "in country" for one month, and as the FNG, or "fucking new guy," was likely assigned that job. Following somewhere in line were two more riflemen: Bill Smith, a twenty-year-old from Heflin, Alabama, and Carl Green, from Seaside, Oregon, twenty-one years old and already wounded twice. Both had been in-country for over half a year. In the middle of the column would have been Harvey Sixkiller, a Native American from Oklahoma, carrying the M60 machine gun, with a few months of his year tour done. And also in the middle would have been Sergeant Bull, a twenty-one-year-old Nebraskan, whose one-year tour of duty was to be over in ten days. On his heels would have been his radio-telephone operator, Richnell, a taciturn twenty-year-old Texan. He and Sixkiller had joined the platoon at the same time and were close friends.

Two other riflemen of the squad were not with them. Bill Preston was on R and R in Thailand -- a one-week "rest and recuperation" leave of which every soldier in Vietnam received at least one -- and Jerry Morehouse was left in Chris wearing flip-flops to heal his trench foot. In the watery Mekong Delta, trench foot was a common problem with a single cure: leaving your feet free to the air until the skin healed.

The six moved single file down a road that led along a medium-sized river to a small, primitive village, one with no electricity and with animals penned underneath the one-room houses. On the far side of the village they stopped on a rice-paddy dike and sat quietly in line, waiting the few minutes left before nightfall. After nightfall, the plan called for them to move one more time, to their assigned night ambush position, somewhere farther down the paddy dike. This final move was to make sure no one in the village could know where their final position would be. A villager who knew could alert the Viet Cong, who could then mortar their position. The villager might himself or herself be a VC.

The final move never took place. A roaring explosion from close to the patrol sent thousands of pellets and metal fragments flying into the men. Lauzon and Smith and Bull were instantly killed, and Green was thrown into the rice paddy with both legs blown off. Richnell and Sixkiller, unhurt, must have flattened out on the dike and returned fire in the direction of the explosion, but with no real targets in sight. Either Richnell or Sixkiller called Chris on the radio, telling them an ambush had killed three and wounded one. One or both of the other squads of third platoon arrived shortly, set up a perimeter, and called in a Medivac chopper. The three dead and Green were airlifted out, and the platoon policed up the four men's weapons and moved back to Chris.

Green died seven days later in the hospital: the wounds that earned him his third Purple Heart were fatal.

This small, deadly ambush was not particularly remarkable in April of 1969. The four men of C-5th-of-the 12th killed in it were a small fraction of the 847 combat deaths suffered that April by U.S. forces in Vietnam. In some ways, though, they were representative of all of those killed. Their ages were close to the most-common age of death of U.S. soldiers killed in action in Vietnam: twenty years. And they were from small towns, and they were draftees.

But the ambush was important for me. Their deaths made room for me in what would become my new family for 1969: Third Platoon, C 5/12, 199th LIB. I would carry one of their M16's.

Chapter One

An Education

Signing up

When people ask me how I ended up in Vietnam, I tell them it was because I got in a fight with my father over money.

It was the summer of 1968. After I had finished my first year of college that June, I had remained in Lansing, Michigan to work on the assembly line at the Oldsmobile factory. I made more than twice the wage I had earned back home in Baltimore the previous summer working construction, and my parents agreed with my argument that I could wind up with more money by the end of the summer if I stayed in Lansing.

I returned home in August when the plant closed down for a few weeks to re-configure the assembly line for the next year's model. After dinner the first night, my dad wanted to know how much money I had saved for the next year of college. I explained that I hadn't saved any just yet -- I had incurred up-front expenses like a motorcycle for getting to work and expenses because of my skydiving hobby. But I thought I would save some in the few weeks before school I would work once the plant restarted.

My dad was angry. He said he and my mom didn't have enough money to pay for the Fall quarter if I had nothing to contribute. I was mad because I thought he was being his usual cheap self. He said he wouldn't give me more money. I said he wouldn't have to -- I would drop out of school for a term and work at Oldsmobile through the Fall.

The next day, August 20, after my Dad had gone to work, I borrowed our second car and headed to our Draft board to find out what would happen to my student deferment while I took off a quarter. Even though we lived in a suburb close to the Baltimore city line, our draft board was in Reisterstown, still a small town mostly surrounded by farms. The Board was in the Masonic Lodge, which looked like something out of a Norman Rockwell painting, with its tall Grecian or Roman pillars facing the town square. Inside I found the office, an old high-ceilinged room with large windows. A solitary white-haired woman appeared to be in charge.

I explained to her my plan to drop out of college until next January, and asked her whether my 2-S deferment would stay in place for this short spell.

In a very cheerful and grandmotherly way, she explained to me that it would not. In fact, she went on to say, I might be drafted during that time. She told me she knew what the monthly call-ups were going to be for each month up to January. She then looked at lists which had all the registered draft-age men with no deferment in our district. She ran her finger down the list, stopped, and turned to me with another big grandmotherly smile.

"Well, you will be drafted in November."

I contemplated that for a few seconds.

"Are you sure?"

"Very. And that's too bad, because if you are drafted in November, you will be in Basic Training during Christmas. But if you want to be home for Christmas, you could volunteer for the draft and we would call you up in October. Basic training takes eight weeks, so you would be home for leave on Christmas"

At this point, you might think I would have left the draft board and taken some time to rethink my plan. Perhaps I could have tried to make do with less money during the school year, or get more work-study hours. Or go back to my father and see if he could find some way to find more money -- I knew my mother would lobby on my behalf.

Instead, without hesitation, I volunteered for the draft.

My first year of college had been exciting -- staying out as late as I wanted, drinking my first beer (my mother and father were teetotalers, so I'd never had an alcoholic drink), discovering that women liked that I was smart, and even taking classes that I enjoyed, everything from poetry to physics. But I had always thirsted for new experiences. I had driven cars too fast, taken up skydiving as soon as I graduated from high school, loved riding motorcycles. Over the summer I worked at Oldsmobile, I had experimented with marijuana and LSD.

During that first year of college, a former artillery officer and I played bridge in the grill at my dorm. How was Vietnam? I wanted to know.

"Not too bad, a lot of boredom," he responded. But he seemed older, wiser, and mature: all, I inferred, from having been in a war.

And at keggers on weekends, a frequent attendee was a fellow who allegedly was the lone survivor of his Marine squad, all the rest having been killed in an ambush. He acted wild, a little out of control, and had what I thought of as a crazy glint in his eyes. What had he seen that so changed his life?

And there was my family. My mother's brother Sam had been killed in combat in World War II. His Purple Heart and the letter of consolation from President Roosevelt hung in the center of the living room wall in my grandparent's house, where it may have been the only thing hanging on a wall. The family talked lovingly of all the wonderful memories they had of Sam: mischievous Sam stealing the Model T and going for a joyride, popular Sam with his many girlfriends, full-of-energy Sam who would come home and bake a cake and eat it all himself. Only later did I find out about heartache my grandparents endured following his death: there were years in which my grandmother was so distraught she could not carry out the daily tasks of caring for her retarded son.

My cousin Douglas, whom I competed with for the approval of the men of the family -- farmers impressed by an aptitude for hunting and fishing and hard manual labor -- was joining the marines. We shared a deep emotional bond despite some differences in our upbringing: his father, my Uncle Walter, was crazy and denigrated book learning, while my parents encouraged it, even exalted it. We were both children of hard, working-class Southern fathers and warm, loving mothers. We learned together how to harden our hearts as we were taught to hunt. We were the apple of our gregarious, caring, maternal grandfather's eye -- a useful antidote to our stern fathers. At some level, I did not want Douglas to be the lone grandson to experience war.

So when the grandmotherly clerk in the Reisterstown Selective Service office suggested I volunteer for the draft so I could be home from Basic for Christmas, I signed up to be inducted on October 17th.

I'm not sure if I thought I would be getting the full war experience, but I knew I was jump-starting my life. I think I thought I was going to be working with missiles, or radar, or military intelligence. I was, after all, pretty smart: I was a National Merit semifinalist, had scored 1570 on the SAT, and had been viewed throughout school as intelligent if a bit underachieving. Would not the military find me a job that would use my talents -- one not so dangerous as infantry that would let me don the mantle of veteran?

And so I drove home, and at the dinner table that night I casually told my parents I had volunteered for the draft and would be inducted October 17th. To my surprise, my mother burst into tears – and not sniffles, but full-blown weeping. I do not remember my father's response clearly, except that he indicated I had made a big mistake that I could and should somehow undo. Their fearful response gave me the first inkling that I had indeed made a mistake.

But I was a narcissistic nineteen-year-old, and I really did want to be drafted. I envisioned returning home two years later, having experienced things my fellow college-goers wouldn't have, things that would make me interesting and mysterious and attractive to women, even if I had been working in the safe environs of missile defense or military intelligence. My relatives would respect me more, and Douglas and I would be on equal footing before them.

In retrospect, I wonder at the cheerfulness of the woman who enrolled me. Did she know to what she was sending me and all those other young men? Wouldn't a wince of discomfort across her face have been more appropriate? Even the many hard men of the Army I would later encounter showed some compassion about the fates they knew awaited us.

On October 17th, my dad drove me to the Armed Forces Examining and Entrance Station on Dundalk Avenue in Baltimore, the neighborhood we had first lived in when we moved there from Virginia eighteen years earlier. He was by now reconciled to the fact that he had a headstrong son who, for better or worse, would be spending the next two years in the armed forces.

Induction was the first experience that hinted at the change in my life to come. The people in my life had treated me consistently as someone with value: my teachers listened respectfully to me and rewarded my accomplishments; my coaches made it clear they thought I had a talent for sports; my family encouraged me in all my activities; my church embraced me as another member of that family.

The Army immediately made it clear it would not treat people as valued members of society. Inductees were yelled at to get in this line or that one, put your urine in that bottle and place it here! Is anyone missing all their fingers and all their toes? Take off your clothes -- yes, all of them, now! Bend over in line, pull your buttocks apart! We took the oath of induction, and before the morning was over, two of us had been taken by the Marines, which left the rest of us with a feeling of relief that it wasn't us. The rest were herded onto buses and told we were going to Fort Bragg, North Carolina.

I was nervous, so I looked for someone I knew, or at least someone with whom I shared something in common. Fortunately, I and a fellow from my neighborhood, who I knew only by reputation, had adjacent service numbers: US51675125 for me and US 51675126 for him. This meant we had begun processing together. As we filled out paperwork and were poked and prodded, we sized each other up as more or less kindred spirits. Then we settled in to the bus for the long ride to Fort Bragg, our last Army ride in a nice, privately-owned bus with cushioned seats, lighting, and a bathroom.

My new friend, Barry Scherr, had wiry hair, a Roman nose, and a perpetual grin. Our neighborhood was perhaps 75% Jewish, as was Barry. As we in the neighborhood grew into high school and became interested in girls, we had become more segregated between Jew and Gentile. But Barry and I still knew a number of people in common.

He had a reputation as a pool shark and general hustler. As we rolled down I-95, he and I discussed people we both knew, how the Orioles had done that season, and the motorcycles we'd owned. Barry told me his dad owned a string of electronics stores and his uncles were in construction. Eventually, Barry suggested we play some gin rummy, and I readily agreed. I had misspent a lot of college time playing cards, and thought myself capable. We played for quite a few hours, with each of us winning some and losing some, but with me holding a slight edge. At this point, Barry suggested we play for money -- a penny a point. I declined. I knew of his reputation as a pool shark and foresaw a hustle. This ended our card game, and the rest of the trip was spent in talk about what we thought lay ahead.

Fort Bragg, home of the airborne: I think we were a little nervous that we would be training with paratroopers. After riding all night in the bus, we arrived at the Army Reception Station at Fort Bragg. We were herded into a big hall, lined up alphabetically by last name (the Army's method of organizing people for any task) and began undergoing a series of tests. Our blood pressures and body temperatures were recorded, we sat for the Armed Forces Qualifying Test, a sort of SAT, and an officer's aptitude test ("would you rather: 1, sit at home and watch television, 2, read a book, 3, play tennis, or 4, crawl through a swamp hunting alligators?" Number 4 appears to have been the "correct" answer, because I didn't choose it and wasn't asked to go to OCS). At some point, we were all lined up alongside one edge of a square field, which I eventually learned was a parade ground. An unfriendly-looking older sergeant stood in front of us. He barked (everybody in charge of a group in the Army barked -- not a shout, or a yell, but a loud, staccato burst of commands):

"All of you college boys, take one step forward!"

About a third of the line stepped forward. I did not: one year of college did not make me a "college boy," I thought.

The sergeant continued: "All the rest of you, stay there and watch. We're going to have these smart college boys show you how to pick up cigarette butts. Now you college boys, move out in line and pick up every cigarette butt you see."

College boys were "the other" in the enlisted man's "regular" army. The "regular" army comprised non-officers who were making the Army their career -- "lifers," as we conscripted soldiers learned to call them. A lifer was distinguished be the "RA" prefix on his service number, which was a number every soldier had that functioned much like a social security number. If you were drafted, your prefix was "US," which we said stood for "unwilling soldier." Lifers took every opportunity to show disdain for non-lifers. And college boys seemed a particularly hated group. Because graduate-school deferments had been abolished that fall, about a third of our inductees were college graduates. We all still wore civilian clothes, and apart from being bossed around much like at the Induction Center, we had not been exposed to the culture that was the Army. But this was the beginning.

That night we slept on bunks in a big hall. The next morning was Sunday, and we were told anyone who wanted to go to church could do so. Then a speaker tried to get us to enlist for a three-year tour of duty instead of the two we were facing as inductees. The pitch was straightforward: enlist for a three-year-hitch, and the Army guarantees you a "school," like radar technician -- something a lot safer than the infantry. The deal had few takers. Only later would I realize what a bargain had been offered. But even after only two days in the Army, I had begun obsessing over minimizing my time of enlistment. No one seemed to value me as an important person. I didn't like that.

Sunday afternoon we were herded to what we were told was the Enlisted Man's club and told we had two hours to enjoy it. A pool table beckoned, and people began calling "first," "second," and so forth, getting their spot in the queue to play. Barry Scherr was maybe sixth or seventh.

We all crowded around the table. As the first people started to play, Barry mercilessly heckled them, making fun of their abilities: "You missed that shot? You're terrible!" This was so inappropriate that guys began to shush him. But he kept it up, getting under people's skin. By the time he took his turn at the table, against a fairly competent fellow who had held the table for most of the rounds, the crowd was unanimous in their distaste for Barry. Even I as his new friend was uncomfortable.

Play started, and Barry was obviously good. But at the end of the game, he rattled the eight ball around a pocket, leaving it just in front of the pocket for his opponent to easily sink and win the game. The crowd jeered and whooped.

Barry turned and quickly said, "Hey, if you guys think you're so good, I'll play anybody for five dollars with two-to-one odds, and I'll play one-handed."

A gangly, pimple-faced seventeen-year-old from West Virginia quickly came to the front and accepted. Clearly he could not believe anyone could be so stupid.

The game started, and ended as soon as Barry had his first turn: he ran the table. Like everyone else, I was shocked, even though I knew Barry was a pool hustler of some renown back in Baltimore. But the amazing thing was that, with his permanent grin and non-stop patter, Barry got the crowd in his corner -- got everyone thinking it was a pretty amazing feat and good fun. He did keep the seventeen-year-old's money, I noticed.

Chapter Two

Basic Training

The introduction

After a few days we were loaded into buses -- not the comfortable Greyhound types we had been shipped in to Fort Bragg, but green-painted school buses -- and driven a short way to a road lined with a small number of drill sergeants. I think we knew they were drill sergeants even then, by their wide-brimmed hats and by their posture: legs spread shoulder-width, chests and chins jutting, hands clasped behind their backs. When the buses stopped, and the driver opened the door, a couple of the drill instructors jumped into the bus, one running down the aisle and the other staying at the front, leaving a passage from the bus to the open door.

"Move, move, get your motherfucking lazy asses out of this bus!" they screamed. The one who had come down the aisle began grabbing people by their shoulders and flinging them into the aisle, pushing them forward. The one at the front gave each troop, as we were soon to be called, a kick in the back to hurry him down the steps and outside. Once we were outside, other DI's screamed at us:

"Move, move, get up that hill, you sorrrrry motherfuckers!"

They motioned us up a short hill towards a set of barracks: four plain, square wooden buildings, totally uniform in size, shape, building material, and color. At the top of the hill, more DI's, and now a couple of what even then we recognized as officers, continued screaming at us to form into a line, roughly shoving the slower-moving troops into place.

Within moments, all of us were lined up between two barracks, facing a raised platform on which the two officers stood. One of the DI's barked instructions to us to file right to what we learned was the supply building, where we were asked what size we were, then given boots and uniforms, down to underwear and socks, all of which we were told to put inside a duffel bag we also were given. Then more yelling, telling us to get back in line at our initial position.

We were now maybe a hundred and forty in number, still in civilian clothes, but lined up in four rows, with our new, filled duffel bags at our sides. A skinny young officer -- a second lieutenant, we were to learn, fresh out of OCS school -- growled at us that a sergeant would be calling out our last names, and that we were to "sound off, loud and clear" with our first name and middle initial.

"Anderson!" the sergeant called. "Everett, L!" came the reply. And down the alphabet the sergeant continued with the call and response, coming closer and closer to my name. Finally:

"Driskill!"

I was not scared, but certainly I was anxious. I was a long way from the world in which I was a loved and valued member.

"Robert, A!" I called, but the "A" came out as a high-pitched screech as my voice broke.

Silence for a moment. Finally the lieutenant mimicked my response, capturing perfectly my breaking voice, leading to some laughter from the troops and the sergeants.

"Are you a girl, Driskill?" the lieutenant asked. "Drop down and give me twenty push-ups."

A chance to redeem myself! I could do twenty pushups, maybe fifty if I had too. I quickly dropped down and started knocking them out. As I effortlessly got to about seventeen, the lieutenant barked:

"When are you going to start, Driskill? You have to count them out loud enough for us to hear you!"

Well, OK, I thought. No problem. And I started again, sounding off loudly (and deeply) as I did each one: "One, two, three..."

Then, as it became clear I was going to get the twenty done, I saw in my peripheral vision one of the DI's approach my side and then throw my duffle bag on my back. I sagged and began to struggle to get the last few done. The call and response then continued down the alphabet, while the DI stood over me, making sure I struggled through the last pushups.

Back on my feet, with the last member of our company having sounded off with first name and middle initial, the second officer on the platform stepped forward. His assured stride announced to all that here was the boss. He was in fact the company commander, a tall, lean Captain, with a face that reflexively formed into a smile when he was not talking. He really did love his job, I came to believe, and his life as an Airborne Ranger.

"Men, I am Captain Reynolds, Commander of C Company, Seventh Training Battalion, and it is my privilege to train you to be soldiers. You are here at the home of the Airborne. This means you will have the best training available." He went on to introduce the skinny lieutenant as his second in command, and then to introduce the Drill Instructors, who were standing in what we would learn was the parade rest stance: feet spread shoulder width, arms clasped behind the back, shoulders back, looking straight ahead. All of the Drill Instructors except one, we were told during their introductions, had served at least one, sometimes two, tours in Vietnam. Sergeant Thompson, whom I soon found out would be the DI for my platoon, had fought in the Ia Drang Valley and had earned a second purple heart as he awaited a Medivac in the midst of that battle. I had no idea then that this had been an early and bloody battle, one later to be immortalized in the book *They Were Soldiers Once, and Young* and the movie of the same name. But I did know, even then, that these Drill Instructors had had real combat experience, which gave them credibility in our eyes. They were also all airborne troops. I had jumped out of a plane about 70 times and was not particularly impressed by that accomplishment. But I knew that airborne troops were elite, and had undergone training that tested their toughness more than taught them how to jump out of a plane -- a skill, like some others taught in the Army, that was no longer useful on the battlefield.

We seldom saw the Captain after that. Once in a while he would show up at one of our training experiences and talk briefly with us, always wearing that big, somewhat feral, smile, and always encouraging us to spend the extra three weeks of harassment that constituted "going airborne."

The other important introduction the Captain made was to our First Sergeant. He was a wiry black man with a wolfish face. Unlike the Captain, he would be with us throughout our training, forever telling us that we were "Sorrrry individuals," weak and incompetent, who would never make decent soldiers. While we eventually came to view most of our platoon-level DI's as men who truly wanted to prepare us for the dangerous and different reality of a wartime army, the First Sergeant was a true misanthrope who eventually quarreled even with my own platoon DI over a medical issue about my own well-being.

At about this time, one of our group farther down the line from me was approached by a DI and told to remove his sunglasses. The fellow took a step forward and turned his back on the DI.

"I'm not doing this," he said.

The DI screamed something at him, grabbing his shoulders. The recruit shoved back. In an instant, three DI's grabbed him and pushed and pulled and dragged him into the small Headquarters hut at the end of the line. We heard shouts, and things hitting the inside walls of the hut, and finally the recruit came flying out of the building, knocking the screen door off of its hinges. His face was bloody and he was moaning. One DI dragged him back into the building, and the other two dusted themselves off and returned to stand in front of our shocked faces, straightening up their uniforms. They glared at us, as did the First Sergeant, the Captain, and the Lieutenant. The First Sergeant barked at us:

"This is what happens if you think you don't have to do what we tell you to. Your mama's not here to take care of you anymore. You are in the ARMY now -- your asses are ours for the next eight weeks."

In a few minutes, an ambulance pulled up, and the Sunglass Guy was removed on a stretcher. What had I gotten into?

The routine

We were then broken down into platoons of about 40 and handed over to our Platoon Drill Instructors. Our DI was thin, very black, with high cheekbones. We knew from the company formation that he was a combat veteran. His voice was not deep, but a little gravely and always loud. He took us to our World War II vintage barracks. It consisted of a large open bay filled with bunk-beds with footlockers at each end; a latrine notable for having no stalls, either for toilets or showers (never a private moment was to be had in the bathroom); and one small separate room. We were assigned bunks (by alphabetical order, of course), and then training began.

Our Drill Instructor taught us how to make up our bunk beds -- first by demonstration, then by ripping off the bedding again and again if the way we did it failed to meet his standards. He taught us how to maintain our clothing and gear in our footlockers: socks rolled just so, brass belt buckle shined, boots polished and aligned, and so on. Everything we possessed had one and only one spot in our footlocker; every piece of clothing or soap or a toothbrush or a razor had a place. There was no room for any personal flare.

We were formed into squads, and our DI picked the biggest member of our platoon and appointed him Platoon Leader. The Platoon Leader got the little private room, but was in charge of making sure everything ran smoothly. In particular, he had to make sure the barracks was ready for inspection every morning, and make sure we had a "fire guard" walking through the barracks at all times during the night. He was, in general, the second in command to the DI.

The DI told us the basics of our schedule: Wake up at 4:30. Clean the barracks. Leave the barracks at 6:00 and form into two columns. March to the mess hall. Climb hand-over-hand along the rungs of a set of a horizontal ladders hung seven feet high. Enter the hall for breakfast. Then it was back to a company formation in the area between the barracks, where First Sergeant asked who wanted to go on sick call:

"Any sorrrry individuals who are going on sick call? You go on sick call and you miss training. You miss training, you may have to do Basic Training allllll over again. Any of you limp dicks going? I know you are just trying to get out of training. I will be watching you!"

His voice became more and more shrill as he inveighed against any goldbricking troop who chose sick call over staying with the platoon during the training day. And any soul with the temerity to go up and say they were going on sick call was ridiculed and threatened: "I'm watching you! You better be *dying*! You are a goldbricking sorrrry motherfucker!"

Needless to say, most of us were truly intimidated. But many days, apparently impervious to the attempted shaming and intimidation, Barry Scherr walked up and went on sick call. His shoulder hurt, he would say.

After the sick call ritual, we would undergo various training exercises. Finally, we would be back in our barracks at about 8:00 p.m., lights out at 10:00. Six days a week, and even Sunday was not totally free from impromptu inspections or marching drills.

Our first order of business was learning how to dress: what to tuck in, how to blouse our pants in our boots, how to remove the shellac from our brass belt buckles and then shine them with Brasso, and when to take off our helmet-liners—plastic helmets that sat inside a metal helmet, which we were not given-- (inside any building). The second order of business was learning how to march. We had to learn how to "form up" in straight lines which were then used to make up columns, and how to make the appropriate turns: "left face" requiring you to move your left foot back, then swivel 90 degrees, "about face" requiring you to place your left foot behind you and then pivot 180 degrees, "column left" requiring you to plant your right foot as you were moving forward and pivot on that foot 90 degrees to your left, and so forth.

We practiced marching while going first to get our hair buzzed off and then to the PX to buy toothpaste, shoe polish, brass polish, and other things not supplied by the army but necessary for survival in Basic. This trip was also our introduction to the infantryman's low-crawl: a technique in which you lay flat on the ground with your arms bent in front of you and locomoted by moving your elbows and knees crab-like. Once we were issued our rifles, we would cradle the rifle across our elbows as we crawled. This first marching experience was our introduction to low-crawling because we learned that every time any one of us in the marching formation executed a move that our DI disapproved of, he would order us down and make us low-crawl a hundred feet or so. And we hardly went a hundred yards before the DI would find something to disapprove of.

Apart from the low-crawling interruptions, marching became one of the most pleasurable parts of army training. The DI marched alongside of us, and led us in call-and-response cadence-keeping chant.

DI: "*I want to be an airborne ranger.*"

Our choral response: "*I want to be an airborne ranger.*"

DI: "*Live a life of blood and danger.*"

Our response: "*Live a life of blood and danger.*"

Him: "*Sound off!*"

Us: "*Sound off!*"

Him: "*One, two, three, four, one-two, three-four.*"

Us: "*One, two, three, four, one-two, three-four.*"

Or:

"*Ain't no use in looking down.*
Ain't no discharge on the ground."

Other chants had been designed to reinforce the fact that there was no going back:

"*Ain't no use in going home,*
Jodie's got your girl and gone." (My girl had, in fact, saved me this concern by dumping me just before I left for Basic).

And the recurrent attempt to make you think a world where life is tenuous is not so strange, by singing about parachute jumping:

"*If my 'chute don't open wide,*
I've got another one by my side,
If that one too fails the test,
Bury me in the leaning rest."

But it was enjoyable to march to cadence, singing as we went. Some songs simply appealed to our adolescent sense of humor:

"*I don't know but I've been told*
Eskimo pussy's might cold."

It was maybe the best part of training, other than the associated low-crawling. Other early training introduced us to PT: physical training. We ran (mostly in formation), we low-crawled, and we swung from rung to rung along the horizontal ladders. These, we were told, would all be things we would do in a final PT test that we had to pass to graduate from Basic. We would have to run a mile in less than something like 8.5 minutes, cross thirty-six ladder rungs without falling, low-crawl a certain distance in less than a certain amount of time, do a "shuttle run" in less than a certain amount of time, and carry another recruit in a fireman's carry for 150 yards. At the start of training, some recruits were daunted by this. I felt confident I could pass, but knew I was weak on the ladder rungs -- we did it every day before meals, and each time I failed to do the seventy-two rungs that would yield the maximum score.

We were also introduced to KP: "kitchen patrol," one of the worst parts of Basic. Every day, three platoon members, picked as always by order in the alphabet of first letter of last name, were ordered to report to the Mess Hall the next morning-at 3:30 a.m. There we met the petty tyrants who ruled the kitchens: cooks. We washed dishes and pots and pans, only to be told to do them again: "Still greasy, you sorry dicks!" We peeled potatoes, served food, scrubbed floors, moved boxes, and generally served as slaves to the people I learned later were pulled for the job of cook from the lowest quintile of the Armed Forces Qualification Test. They relished their control over us. We would return to the barracks around midnight. Those of us with names that started with letters early in the alphabet, like me, got an extra helping of KP as we started the alphabet anew.

And so our early days included marching to classes on the Uniform Code of Military Justice—the Army's legal code—and to classes on military organization -- what were the various ranks, who and how to salute -- interspersed with inspections of our barracks and our uniforms, which we invariably failed, leading to low-crawling or two-mile runs, and with PT.

But we were in the Army. Our basic function was to kill. So within a week or so we were issued rifles. Despite the fact that if we ended up in Vietnam we would use the plastic-stock, fully-automatic M-16 rifle, we were issued the M-14 rifle: a semi-automatic weapon with a wooden stock, which was significantly bigger and heavier than the M-16. Like marching, a technique not used in combat since Napoleon, weapons training was not about learning something directly applicable to combat, but rather learning habits of thought and behavior that might help us in combat situations.

Before ever firing our weapon, we spent hours learning how to care for it: how to clean it and to take it apart and put it back together rapidly. We learned how to march with the M-14, how to low-crawl with it, and how to run with it.

Our rifles gave our DI's an additional tool for teaching us to march. The standard marching protocol called for each of us to carry our rifle leaned against the right shoulder, with the butt held in the palm of the hand. But often our marching was faulty, as when the command would be "Column left!" and someone in the column would turn right. Now our DI's would make us carry our rifles over our shoulders by holding the barrels in our hands, with the heavy wooden stock sticking out behind. When someone turned the wrong way, his rifle stock would swing and hit the head of the person next to him.

Looking back, I realize how perfect this system was for fulfilling one of the aims of Basic Training: to teach us that the member of the group who made the mistake did not suffer the direct consequences, but his fellow squad members did. All of our early training had an element of this: when an individual screwed up, we all low-crawled, we all dropped and did pushups. But the swinging rifle butts were practically genius in how they spared the individual who made the mistake but made others pay.

In some sense, all of our early training pushed us to form a tight bond at the platoon level. We all quickly came to hate the army, especially as personified in our Drill Instructor, whom we could never please, and who arbitrarily made our lives miserable. For example, one Saturday night early in the training cycle, our DI showed up at the barracks around midnight, had us fall out into the road between the barracks, and start low-crawling, then had us do pushups, then more low-crawling, more pushups, and on and on for an hour.

So most of us tried to help each other out. Some became leaders, who might intervene in the fights that broke out -- living in our conditions, even friends could become enormously irritated with each other. And some were better adapted to the constant harassment, lack of time to ourselves, and an uncertain and potentially dangerous future, and encouraged us because they seemed so confident that we would all get used to it.

Our best example of this was Thomas Dillow, also known, he told us, as "TD" and "Top Dog," and "Chickenkiller." He was a stocky, muscular West Virginian who talked non-stop, mostly about cunnilingus. "Know why I always have this penny in my mouth?" he would say. "Because it tastes like pussy." He was missing his two front upper teeth -- "The girls love it, lets me lick their pussy better." And no matter how tired we were, no matter how frustrated, he never stopped entertaining us with tales of his adventures, which all ended up with him eating pussy. He was frequently telling black guys, who universally said about cunnilingus that they didn't eat anything they couldn't grill, that he did not care how big their dicks were, he could steal their women because he would eat their pussy. And no matter how many times we low-crawled, or did pushups, or forced marches, TD never looked bothered.

Barry Scherr was another example. Every evening he would talk endlessly about life back in Baltimore, regaling us with tales from pool halls and night clubs. And he seemed untouched by the attempts to shame him for going so often on sick call. He told us, as the weeks went by, that he was slowly beginning to convince a doctor that an old motorcycle accident had so damaged his shoulder that he could not possibly do regular, physically-demanding training.

And gradually, some things began to change. For one, we were now spending more time really learning things rather than merely being harassed. In particular, once we had learned how to clean and care for our rifle, we were taken to the rifle range and taught the Army way of shooting. I looked forward to this, because I had always been a crack shot with a rifle -- something which had always impressed my relatives.

The Army way involved shooting from a prone position (flat on one's belly, legs spread, elbows planted to make sure our arms provided a secure platform for the rifle), a sitting position (legs bent at 45 degrees in front of us, with elbows locked onto knees to again provide a secure platform), and a standing position, also called "offhand" shooting (legs spread shoulder width, left arm extended to hold the rifle beneath the barrel, and right elbow cocked and horizontal to the ground, with right hand grasping the pistol grip just below the trigger). Many of my fellow recruits had never shot a weapon before. The instructors taught how to use and adjust the sights (iron sights-not telescopic, with a small post attached at the end of the barrel which you lined up over the target and in line with a v-shaped notch in the rear sight, close to your eye). They taught us how to position the body, how to slow our breathing as we prepared to pull the trigger without jerking. We practiced by shooting at human silhouettes downrange at various distances up to 300 yards. It was a good way to spend a day for me, because I seldom got yelled at: I knew how to shoot.

As we collectively got better at shooting, we approached an important day: the day we zeroed our weapons. Rifles all have slight variations between where the sights tell you the bullet will hit and where the bullet will actually, consistently hit. Zeroing your weapon means that you shoot consistently enough that you can tell in what direction your sights are off. So if, when aiming at a bull's-eye target your bullets are consistently down and to the left from the bull's-eye center, then you can adjust your sights, using tiny controls on the sights that allow you to move them. That way, when you line up your sights on the bull's-eye, you hit it.

But what was necessary to do this was an ability to consistently shoot bullets into the same spot. This is where being a good shot came into play. If every time you pulled the trigger, the bullet did not consistently go to close to the same spot, then you could not figure out what adjustment to make to your sights.

Zero Day was an unusually cold day for November in North Carolina. The Drill Instructors had made it a competition to see which of the four platoons in our company would be first to have all its weapons zeroed: the winning platoon was to go to the Enlisted Men's club that night (for the first time ever to be free of the barracks when not going to a training site) to drink beer. Additionally, as soon as you zeroed your weapon you were allowed to go to a tent with heater inside and lounge the rest of the day. This sounded like a small heaven.

And as I anticipated, I was one of the first to zero my rifle. To the loud, command-voice accolades of my DI, I walked down the range behind the others trying to get zeroed and went to the heated tent, joining a handful of other sharpshooters. We warmed up, congratulated ourselves, and settled in for a first: a lazy, comfortable day.

But I was to learn an important lesson: the Army is not based on fairness. Soon a truck pulled up, and that day's KP slaves started unloading canisters of hot food: lunch for the company, as many troops would take the full day to successfully zero their weapon. Then a mess-hall sergeant entered our tent, scanned the few of us in there, and said: "You, you, and you, come with me." I was one of the "you's," and I had a sinking feeling we were going to the mess hall as KP replacements. As I began to grasp, the day's scheduled KP slaves also needed to zero their weapons.

Back we went to the mess hall, where we served the rest of the day. I watched as my platoon, the competition winner, went through for supper, anticipating their later trip to the Enlisted Men's club for beer, while I washed pots and pans until midnight. No, my DI did not intervene on my behalf. As I was learning, this was the Army way.

The change

At about five weeks, we could sense a real change in how we were being treated: not as much seemingly meaningless harassment, such as when the DI would walk by me during PT while I did leg raises, and kick my stomach, saying, "You're weak, Driskill." And our DI began to engage us as real people during training. One afternoon, as we worked again on dismantling and reassembling our rifles, our DI, instead of walking around demeaning us for our efforts, simply walked around, silently giving us approving looks. He even engaged in conversation that suggested he was interested in our lives:

"Dillow!"

"Yes Drill Sergeant!"

"Why do they call you Chickenkiller?"

"Drill Sergeant, I can't help it if they die when I fuck them!"

And one day, after a low-crawl practice for our PT test, our DI noticed that the knees of my pants were bloody, as they had been after every low crawl for weeks. But this time he made me show him my knees, scowled, and told me in no uncertain terms that I was to report for sick call the next day.

When I did so that next morning, the First Sergeant as usual began calling me a sorrrrry individual, a goldbricker, someone who would face his anger when I later returned. But to my surprise my DI intervened, telling the First Sergeant that I wasn't a malingerer and my knees were infected. He and the First Sergeant actually had a spat: the First Sergeant insisted my knees were fine, while my DI, in a scornful tone, told the First Sergeant, who outranked him, that he wasn't mindful enough of the recruits' health.

Things were changing.

Finally, one Saturday afternoon after training was over, our DI followed us into the barracks. This time, instead of carrying out what I thought of as his "strafing run," in which he arbitrarily selected problems with our cleaning and had us do pushups as punishment, he gathered us around. He explained that the first five weeks had had a very specific purpose: to make us forget about civilian life and prepare us for the life we might be facing, a life of combat in which random bad things happened. To survive, we would need to believe we could persevere, and not, as he said, "fold your tent."

He went on to explain that the early scene when we first arrived in which a malcontent was beaten up had been staged: the malcontent was a DI from another company who had been acting. And he told us the constant harassment was in fact sometimes unrelated to any mistakes on our parts: it was just part of the plan. He gave us passes for the EM club for that night and told us that if we could "keep our shit together," a weekend pass might be in our future.

So our lives became less miserable. We did get a weekend pass and went to Fayetteville. There I learned the secret of Tommy Dillow's success with women: he didn't care what they looked like. Our days still began at 4:30, we still had KP duty, but low-crawling and pushups became rare. We spent our days learning how to engage in hand-to-hand combat, as well as how to use gas mask (and had to spend a minute without a mask in a room filled with tear gas), and a bayonet.

Like marching, the bayonet had not been militarily useful in a long time, maybe since the First World War. But we practiced thrusting and parrying, and we sounded off in unison to the drill sergeant's shouted question:

"What is the spirit of the bayonet?"

"To kill!"

And about this time Barry Scherr showed up in the barracks after spending the day on sick call. He was waving a sheaf of papers in his hand.

"This is a profile, guys!" he said. "The doctor say I'm not physically able to do regular training. I'm moving to a special training company -- no PT, and no chance of going into the infantry!"

We crowded around and read the profile. Indeed, it said that due to an old motorcycle accident, Barry's left shoulder was too weak to allow him to engage in the physical training in our standard Basic unit. Laughing, he practically skipped out of the building to a pull-up bar that every barracks had outside. He caught the bar one-handed with his left hand, and proceeded to do a dozen or so one-handed pull-ups.

"I fooled them! No infantry for me. In fact, I'll probably get a discharge with disability while you guys are going to infantry training!"

One-handed pull-ups with a "bad" shoulder. Amazing. All the attempts to shame him and humiliate him for going on sick call had failed, and his plan, as we now recognized it, had worked. Remarkably, there was something about his personality that led all of us to applaud his subterfuge.

Finally we went on bivouac, a three day-and-night exercise in which we marched about fifteen kilometers with full packs and rifles, then set up camp with two-man positions, each man providing half of a tent. We dug latrines and foxholes and then did various infantry drills. We learned how to assault an object using cover fire, with squads taking turns advancing while another put down suppressing fire. (We were given blanks to fire, and defenders used blanks also.) We low-crawled with our rifles under barbed wire while live machine gun fire went overhead. And we were taught how to use a compass to navigate across territory from point A to point B. After three days and nights, we were cold and miserable, but almost done with Basic.

The end of the beginning

Last of all came our graduation parade. The entire training battalion marched past a reviewing stand, then returned as a company to the area between our barracks, where I had first answered "Robert, A." There we were told -- alphabetically, of course, and publicly, so all could hear -- our next duty assignment. This would be where we would get our Advanced Training for our particular "MOS:" Military Occupation Specialty. I began to get worried as the drill sergeant went through the A's, B's, and C's, and every single draftee was assigned to Advanced Infantry Training at Fort Polk, Louisiana, MOS Eleven-Bravo. There were more than a few college graduates in the group, whom I'd thought would be sent to a language school, or military intelligence, or missile defense -- one of the MOS's to which I had assumed I would be assigned.

"Driskill: Fort Polk, Louisiana, MOS eleven-bravo."

I was not going to get the military experience "lite," in which I was close enough to it to feel like I had been through something important and defining, but safe. I, and every single draftee except one, were going to Fort Polk, also known as "Tigerland."

By the end of the alphabet our company had grown silent. Looking around, I assumed my expression mirrored those around me: a blank, slack face, with big eyes looking glassy. (I later learned this is what shock looked like.) Our hopes had been dashed. Our fears had been realized.

One of our DI's jumped up on the small platform in front of us. "Listen: all ya'll going to Fort Polk, don't hang your heads. There's only one reason there's an army: this!"

With that, he reached across his shoulder, grasped the powder-blue braided rope that hung in an oval suspended from his shoulder and under his armpit. This, we knew was the symbol of the infantry.

"The Queen of Battle! If you gonna be in this man's army, be in the only part that really matters!"

Our mood lifted somewhat, and in some of the long days that were to follow, his words would generate just enough pride to help me get through.

We were given orders that allowed us to take a bus back to where we were inducted. Barry Scherr and I rode back together, with Tommy Dillow along. Barry did indeed seem to be on his way out of the Army. Tommy Dillow, it turned out, had nowhere to go for the holidays, and talked Barry into letting him come with him. Back home myself, I celebrated a Christmas I cannot remember, and reported to Fort Polk on January 3, 1969, for advanced infantry training.

Wide river

We were treated better in AIT than in Basic: we got up at 5:30 rather than 4:30, we did not do KP, we usually received weekend passes, and some of our officers and sergeants seemed to treat us with a little more dignity.

Along with a collection of Drill Instructors assigned to the company as a whole, each platoon had a "platoon sergeant" who had just graduated from a six-week course designed to turn out newly-minted sergeants. Like us, these so-called "shake-and-bake" sergeants had zero combat experience. They had been through Basic and Advanced Infantry Training, then the 6-week course, and were here to get some seasoning in leadership.

The actual Drill Instructors treated them with respect, but clearly viewed them as trainees: all they knew so far about being a sergeant was "book learning." The DI's had all been in combat, and had come up through the ranks. As a consequence, our "shake-and-bakes" were fairly distant from the DI's and close to being friends with us. I learned after the war that of the four assigned to our company, one was killed in a firefight and one suffered permanent disabilities after throwing a grenade that got hung up close to him in the jungle undergrowth.

Our daily routine was much as it had been in Basic: we cleaned the barracks, started the day with PT, then were marched or trucked to some part of the fort for training. Whenever we marched, we sang one song:

"Wide river, river of Saigon,
One more river to cross, hey!"

And that is how we came to think about our future: one big obstacle to surmount.

We were given the M16 rifle, and trained in its care and use. The M16 was two pounds lighter than the M14, shorter, fired a smaller bullet at higher velocity, and was fully automatic. The semi-automatic M14 fired one bullet per pull of the trigger, while the M16 had a selection button that allowed it to fire continuously as long as you held the trigger. In one early class our instructors told us about what a wonderful weapon we had compared to the AK47, which was the weapon of the Viet Cong/NVA (North Vietnamese Army). Our M16 fired more rapidly on full automatic, and it fired a high-velocity bullet that had great stopping power. But even during training at Fort Polk, we realized that the M16 was a delicate weapon that failed to operate if not kept very clean. And the ammunition clip that fed the rifle held twenty rounds. On full automatic, twenty rounds were expended in what seemed like the blink of an eye, requiring us to pull the empty clip from the rifle, roll to one side (if prone, as we usually were) to extract another clip from a bandolier-like string of cloth clip-holders, then roll back and insert the new clip. But we had not been in combat, and so assumed that we did indeed have the best rifles. We were taught marksmanship with the M16, just as we had been with the M14. On the firing range, we were also taught to use the full-automatic feature to fire three-shot bursts. We were told that recoil would ruin our aim if we fired longer bursts.

But we were also taught that in Vietnam we would mostly fire the weapon from the hip, or else aim it like a shotgun: not lining up front sight with back sight on the target, but quickly swinging the rifle, still held in a traditional position with cheek up against the back of the barrel, and firing a three-shot burst. I cannot remember ever practicing this with real ammunition. Training was still mostly about marksmanship: trying to hit a target with a single carefully-aimed shot at fifty yards, a hundred yards, and two hundred yards.

We also learned how to use the other basic tools of the combat infantryman: how to fire and maintain the M60 machine gun (fully automatic, a heavier, more powerful weapon than the M16 that fired long belts of ammunition and came with a replacement barrel if the first one overheated), how to fire a grenade launcher, how and when to throw a grenade (we practiced throwing a live grenade a few times), how to use the PRC-25 radio-telephone along with map coordinates to call in artillery fire. We learned how to fire a LAW (a shoulder-carried light antitank weapon) and each fired it once, blowing up old trucks a few hundred yards away. And we learned how to set up and fire a claymore mine. This is a roughly 9"- by-12" curved rectangle of C4 explosive perhaps a half-inch thick with many small metal pellets implanted on its concave side. A wire of fifty feet or so connects an embedded blasting cap to a handheld generator that fits in your palm. To fire the mine, simply squeeze the generator a couple of times. The important thing to remember is to set up the concave surface facing away from you. We each set one off in training.

We only learned a few infantry tactics. Primarily, we were taught how to assault an objective, much as we had on bivouac in Basic. We broke our squad into two "fire teams" and moved in tandem, usually through light brush and forest, towards the objective, usually a collection of bunkers on a hilltop. One fire team would lay down suppressing fire at the objective while the other moved from a position of cover -- say, from behind some fallen logs -- up toward other cover closer to the objective.

We also learned how to set up an ambush. The basic ambushes were "in line" and a so-called "L-shaped" ambush. Perhaps, we were told, you have found a jungle trail. If the trail was straight, you would line up your unit in a straight line along the trail, with claymores set up to spray the trail. If an enemy unit came down the trail, you would let them pass until all of them were in the "kill box" -- that is, lined up opposite your unit. Then your M60 machine gun would initiate the ambush by opening fire.

If there were a sharp curve in the trail, though, you would place your squad's machine-gun team, consisting of the machine gunner and one other rifleman who would help keep the belt of ammunition feeding smoothly, so as to form the bottom leg of the "L." Then you would string out the rest of the squad along the trail at a right angle to the bottom leg, along which they set up claymore mines. As with the in-line ambush, you let your biggest weapon, the M60 machine gun, initiate the ambush. The fire from the machine gun rakes along the length of the trail while your fellow soldiers fire their M16's across the trail and detonate their claymores across the trail as well.

And we learned how to set up an NDP -- a night defensive position. You break your platoon into three-man groups and distribute these groups equidistant around a circular perimeter. One man stays on guard for one hour while the other two sleep, and then the second man is woken up to keep guard while the original guard sleeps, and this is rotated like this through the night. The platoon leader -- either a lieutenant or a sergeant, the platoon sergeant if there is one, the medic, and the RTO (radio telephone operator) -- all stay together in the center of the perimeter. They monitor the radio through the night and send in hourly "sitreps:" brief situation reports.

The over-arching lesson we took from all of this was that whenever your unit was in contact with the enemy, you sent the machine gun to the most critical point of the fight. The M60 could fire those long belts of continuous ammunition and suppress enemy fire. The rounds fired were bigger and heavier than those of an M16, and could chew through foliage and even small logs and not-too-deep earth berms.

We also were trained in assaulting from an APC, an armored personnel carrier. These were vehicles that looked like a little metal box set on tracks like those on tanks. A driver sat with his head poking outside the top of the box, and a squad of infantry road in the interior of the box. The assault involved the APC coming to a stop, the rear ramp (which formed one side of the box) being lowered, and the infantry squad running out and attacking the objective.

As with much of our training, we would learn that this never happened in Vietnam. It turned out that the armor on the APC could not stop a direct AK47 round. It could not stop a rocket-propelled grenade, either, which would penetrate the armor, then explode inside the box, sending hot metal fragments throughout that killed all inside. Finally, when mines planted in roads exploded, anyone inside the APC was thrown violently about and ended up dead. Hence, in Vietnam, everyone rode on top of the APC. Why we were not trained about this I do not know. Perhaps, like the proselytization about the M16, the Army did not want to admit to any deficiencies about equipment.

Especially memorable was the lesson on escape and evasion. First our company was told to be very careful when you crossed a road, where the enemy could easily see you. We were then shown how to wring a live chicken's neck to get a nutritious meal from a local farm -- not new to me, as my Dad had done this when we visited his family farm. Then we were told to give only our name, rank, and serial number if we were caught. Finally, as the sun set, we were broken into four-man teams, given a compass and map, and told to reach an objective before morning.

About midnight, our four-man team approached the road that we had to cross. We crept to the edge, looked as carefully as we could, and then broke across. Immediately, "enemy" soldiers jumped up from the roadside, maybe fifty feet from us.

"Halt!" they yelled. "You are now prisoners."

We raced away toward the woods. As I stepped on the road's shoulder, though, I hit a rock or something and badly twisted my ankle. I tried to hobble deeper into the woods, but the enemy soldiers caught me.

They dragged me back to the road and tied a sandbag over my head. I heard a truck pull up, and they shoved me into the back and pushed me flat. We drove off, and a short time later I was pushed out of the truck and onto the ground.

"Get up," one of my captors said.

I stood. A captor on each side grabbed an arm.

"We're taking you to the command post," my original captor said. "Don't try to take off the sandbag."

We shuffled along for a while, then stopped.

"We're at a ditch," I was told, "about three feet across, filled with water. We're going to let go of your arms. After we do, jump as hard as you can to get across the ditch."

They dropped my arms. It was a cold February in Louisiana. We had been cold and wet off and on for almost two months now, and we all hated it. Cold by itself you can deal with, but cold and wet is miserable.

Worried about getting wet, I crouched a bit, swung my arms back to get some momentum, and launched myself as hard as I could -- straight into a wall.

My captors picked me up, turned me around, and dragged me back a few feet, then pushed me through what felt like a door. My nose felt like it was broken. Finally they pulled the sandbag off of my head. I stood in a room, and across from me was our company captain -- a squat, chubby man who was a bit of a martinet -- dressed up as a Viet Cong, conical hat and all.

"What company are you from?" he demanded.

I knew that whatever was in store for me that night, it would be worse if I gave anything but my name, rank, and serial number, which I did.

After a few more attempts, they pushed me down into a kneeling position, put a two-by-four behind my knees, and pushed me back, bending my knees over the board. Again they asked for my company. And while in pain, I still knew my best outcome lay in staying with name, rank, and serial number.

A few more pushes later, they had my initial captors haul me out to a small guarded pen, where they made me hug an upright pole and then cross my legs around it. They then pushed me down to a sitting position on the ground, which turned out to be excruciatingly painful.

"This is the Apache Pole," my captor said. "You'll stay here like this 'til you tell our commander your company."

I could look around now and see that they had constructed a small fake Viet Cong outpost, complete with a palisade wall and my little outdoor prison. My captor stood by the prison gate, smoking.

After a few minutes, our little fake fort was "attacked:" a flare went up, recorded explosive sounds played loudly, and the people in the hut where our captain had interrogated me were running the other way.

I tried to raise up off of the apache pole, but my ankle was too swollen.

The "guard" approached me. "Hey, you're supposed to escape now. See that culvert under the fence? Go! I have to stay here until all the prisoners escape."

"Help me up," I told him. "My ankle is twisted."

He did, and I hobbled off and escaped through the culvert. I then painfully limped to our rendezvous point as dawn broke. They trucked us back to our barracks, whereupon I went on sick call. My ankle was taped, I was freed from PT, and my nose, still bloody, was pronounced unbroken.

We were to find out in Vietnam that our chances of being taken prisoner were extremely slim. In firefights there, chances to surrender did not exist. But perhaps something was gained, again, in reinforcing the idea that the most important survival skill was a commitment to never give up the fight for your life.

A week or so later we graduated from AIT. The only surprise in our orders was that two people in our company did not get sent to Vietnam. One was assigned to an infantry unit in Hawaii, the other to one in Germany. The rest of us, as anticipated, were ordered to report to Fort Ord in California to be transported to Vietnam. We looked around at each other with the certain knowledge that some of us would not survive. I doubt that most of us thought we were going off to save democracy, or to stop communism before it reached our doorstep. If we thought about it at all, I believe, most of us thought that our democratically-elected leaders had decided to send us to fight, and we should go. We wanted to cross that one last river and return to our civilian lives.

We left, I think, not exactly trained to be infantrymen, but having been exposed to a variety of tools and tactics. We would all find that combat involved a lot of on-the-job training.

Chapter Three

Lieutenant Pace

April 21, 1969

Dear folks,

     Just another note to let you know I'm doing fine, and to let you know my address. I just got assigned tonight and drew my weapon. I move to the field Saturday. I'm very pleased with my company.

     The Monsoons have started and it's pretty wet. I guess I'll stay wet for the next six months, but at least it's warm.

     You probably have got the $140 I sent you. If not, let me know. Use it for my bills, etc. Any left, just save. Same with my income tax. I'll probably ask you to send it to me in about 7 or 8 months.

     Nothing much else to say. I'll write as often as possible, but it may be difficult to write often. Write when you get a chance.

Bob

The booby trap

"Sir, I'll take a squad from my platoon!"

I had heard over the radio a squad from First Platoon report to the Captain from a nearby rice paddy:

"Two gooks went into some Nipa palm. There's booby traps everywhere."

They then said they were returning to where our company had set up on an untilled little parcel of dry land, rock-hard and barren of any plant life at the tail end of the dry season, and separated from the rice paddy by a small hedge of Nipa palm and other shrub-like vegetation. Captain Goodwin talked on the radio with Battalion, and then said:

"We're going to have to send another platoon out there and see if we can locate the gooks."

That is when our new Lieutenant made the offer. As he said it, I knew that my first impressions had not been wrong: this was a man who came looking for glory.

It was the late morning of May 20, 1969, still and hot as usual. Five weeks before, I and a planeload of other soon-to-be FNG's (fucking new guys) had walked off a commercial jet into the sweltering wet blanket of a Vietnamese afternoon. Transported in a bus wrapped in crosshatched metal bars to the vast, dusty, vegetation-free Long Binh military base, I was processed into the 199th Light Infantry Brigade. After a week of training, where we reacquainted ourselves with the M16, brushed our teeth with almost-pure fluoride, and got partially acclimatized to the backsweat- and heatstroke-inducing climate, I and two others were sent to our new home: Charley Company, 5th Battalion, 12th Regiment.

The Executive Officer-"the XO", the officer who ran things from the rear back at permanent company headquarters- met us. He was a Second Lieutenant and very informal with us: no salutes, no coming to attention. It was almost like having been hired into a civilian job and meeting your new manager. He issued us our M16's -- just checked out by an armorer, he said, as they had been carried by recent casualties (the ill-fated KIA's of the late Sergeant Bull's ambush squad, I would learn). He also told us a few things about our company: We were ninety-five strong, split into three rifle platoons and one mortar platoon, plus headquarters and a supply sergeant. We'd had five members killed in action so far that year, and the most frequent injuries were from booby traps, typically resulting in losses of feet, hands, and eyes. He said all this as if describing the features of a factory where we would be working. He then showed us where we could stow our duffle bags in the company storeroom -- we would not see them again until, if all went well, we rotated home in 365 days -- and put us on a truck with some older soldiers to carry us to "the field," where the three of us were all to be assigned to Third Platoon.

The truck carried us south toward Saigon. Soon after we left our Brigade Main Base in Long Binh, we approached a small hill to our right, from which grew an orchard-like group of what appeared to be withered trees. As we passed, we could see that the trees were withered because they were burned. And stuck in the blackened limbs were blackened, burned bodies.

"Air strike or artillery caught them a few weeks ago," said one of our fellow passengers. "During the mini-Tet offensive. A massed attack."

Our older and more knowledgeable fellow passenger went on to explain that like the better-known Tet Offensive of 1968, there had been a smaller Tet Offensive this year, complete with massed human-wave attacks. The human-wave attack down this hill had been caught in the open and destroyed by our lethal firepower.

Once I had joined my company, I found that almost everyone in my platoon had passed this way recently, and all had been unnerved by the sight of so many burned bodies. Why, I wondered, were the bodies burned? No one, it turned out, knew for sure. Maybe napalm from an air strike. But some suspected that the artillery rounds that had been used were white phosphorous -- "Willy Peete" -- rounds that were supposed to be used only as markers—artillery rounds that exploded a hundred feet in the air to let the ground troops send back directional adjustments--- before explosive rounds were used during "fire for effect." I was vaguely aware that using white phosphorous to kill people was against the Geneva Convention. But I guessed that in a crisis, like a human wave attack, the Geneva Convention became an unaffordable luxury. I was glad I had missed the "mini-Tet."

We passed through Saigon and rolled on through a watery countryside of rice paddies, rivers, and small primitive-looking villages: w i t h no sign of electricity, the houses we could see seemed to be one-room buildings on stilts, with pigs penned underneath. As night fell, we stopped at what I would learn was the Brigade's forward operating base compound: "The Fishnet," it was called. We were told to sleep in one of the overturned half-cylindrical sandbag-covered bunkers of corrugated metal that dotted a small enclosed area. As I tried to sleep, artillery boomed intermittently and flares illuminated parts of the sky. No one had told us where we were, or why artillery was being fired. I would learn that some of this was fire support for various night patrols, and part "harassing and interdicting" fire that was pre-programmed to land at spots where the Viet Cong were anticipated to be moving through the night. Rats scurried over the loose boards that made up the floor, so I slept sitting up. I was awakened in the middle of the night by a rat climbing on my shoulder. This began my lifelong hatred of rats.

The next morning we arrived at our company base, or "the field" as it was known to people in "the rear." It was a small, sandbag-walled fort covering about half an acre on the side of a river or canal in the Mekong delta southwest of Saigon. A small village was located a few hundred yards down the river. Across the river was another fort, which housed Delta Company. The surrounding landscape was mostly rice paddies: flat, water-filled fields with green shoots of rice sticking up, edged on all sides by small earthen dikes whose tops were about two feet above the water and which were just wide enough to walk on. In the distance we could see small clumps of Nipa palm, which looked like twenty-foot-high ferns.

As I was to learn, our typical routine was to have two of the three rifle platoons go out on nighttime ambush, while the remaining platoon and the mortar platoon guarded the fort. On ambush, the platoon, which consisted of three squads, would simply set up in a line along one of the few dry areas around an area designated by Intelligence as a possible Viet Cong route. Sometimes each squad would move out to a slightly different area. They would set out claymores, and scan the area throughout the night with a starlight scope, a small telescope that enhanced any ambient light and gave a greenish but clear view of the surroundings. In the morning, like as not, they would find that rats had chewed through the claymore wires.

If the platoon had been on night ambush, it generally got to sleep in the fort the next day. But if it had guarded the fort, it would go on patrol, moving through the paddy mud that almost sucked your boots off. Everyone tried to stay off of the paddy dikes as much as possible, for that was where the booby traps were positioned. They were usually set up as a grenade or other explosive round hidden in the grass alongside the dike, with a monofilament tripwire strung across the dike top. But sometimes there was no way to move except along a dike.

As the three FNG's, my two fellow replacements and I were given the most dangerous jobs. Nelson Bunch, who called himself "Stinger," was a black guy over six feet tall from Harlem, and was given an M60 with one of the squads. Ken Handy from Minnesota, blond and fair, was assigned to walk point for another squad. And I had been given the job of RTO for the third platoon Lieutenant. This meant I carried on my back the PRC-25 radio, or as we referred to it, the "Prick 25." It weighed about 25 pounds (although the "25" in its name was because it was the 25th version of that radio), was carried on my back, and kept me within a yard or so of the platoon Lieutenant, because he had to be able to get the handset from me at any moment. The handset, which served as microphone and receiver, hooked on my web gear—a woven belt with suspender-like parts on which you could hook things like grenades-- and had a coiled cord that could stretch maybe two yards from the radio.

Along with the radio itself, I carried a spare battery of a couple of pounds, and all my other gear: my rifle, my ammunition, a claymore, three grenades, and canteens of water. If we were moving any distance for an extended operation, I also carried a pack with C-rations, a poncho liner, an entrenching tool (a folding portable shovel) and the few small personal items (photos, sometimes a camera, maybe a book, or some letter writing material) that we all carried in a waterproof M60 ammunition can. And we all wore flak jackets all the time: heavy vests made out of some material that would, we hoped, stop the shrapnel from booby traps from penetrating our torsos.

Until a few days before May 19th, I carried the radio for Lieutenant Walker (I think that was his name). I remember his name less well than his characteristics. He was a ROTC product (he had been a member of the Reserve Officer Training Corp in college) who was respected by the older platoon members. Comfortable in command, he had an easy familiarity with the platoon, inviting input from the veterans when possible but quick to make a decision when needed. And he openly shared our desire to yes, do our job, but only while maximizing our chances of getting home and returning to civilian life. One night we were sent on a "moving ambush," where we moved at prearranged times from one predetermined ambush site to another. At some point, the whistle of an approaching artillery round sent us all to the ground. A massive and terrifyingly close explosion followed. The Lieutenant grabbed the radio mike and forcefully called Battalion to tell them our location and to tell them to stop firing. The shell, he was told, was preplanned H and I -- harassing and interdicting -- fire. Some officer in charge of alerting Artillery about our movements that night had failed to do his job. A heated exchange followed: Command told him to continue moving to the next location, the artillery mistake would be corrected. The Lieutenant told Command that we were not moving until he heard confirmation that that the mistake was corrected: he wasn't going to have his platoon killed by friendly fire. From the sound of the officer on the other end of the radio, I felt sure that a reprimand would await our Lieutenant at the end of the night. But Lieutenant Walker held his ground, and we waited, prone on a dike, until he got the assurances he wanted.

During the few weeks I was his RTO, I thought we worked together well. I began to anticipate when he would need the handset, and he began to use me as a sounding board for mostly rhetorical questions: "Do you think the Old Man is sending us on ambush tonight?" I was also an emissary: "Tell the squad leaders we should carry at least ten clips tonight on ambush." I liked him and trusted him to try and minimize our danger while doing our job.

And during these weeks we were lucky: we had only one enemy contact, during a night ambush. A column of four Viet Cong crossed by the squad set up at one end of the ambush. We heard the squad open up with their machine gun and M16's. In the morning, they found four dead Viet Cong, and I learned that standard operating procedure was to leave the bodies where they lay. Sergeant Unger, the squad leader, explained to me that the local VC were all members of the local villages, and their relatives would come and police up the bodies.

Across the river from our fort, though, was Delta company, and their experience reminded us that we were in fact lucky. Almost daily, we would hear a distant explosion, and then later the approach of a medivac helicopter. Over the Battalion radio net, I would sometimes here their radio traffic:

"Bravo Five, we have one Whiskey India Alpha, have secured a perimeter, need dust off immediately." We began to refer to the hard-luck company as "Dust-off Delta." I also learned in a couple of other ways that we were indeed lucky.

First, I found out that Stinger, Ken, and I were replacements for the four platoon members who were KIA ("killed in action") during that ill-fated ambush of the seventeenth of April 17 that was the basis of the prologue. I learned this from Jerry "Morehead Sam" Morehouse, who had not been in the ambush: he had immersion foot, more commonly known from the First World War as "trench foot," and had been kept in the fort that night wearing flip-flops to dry out his feet. The two survivors, Harvey Sixkiller and Richnell, never spoke of that night to me, an FNG. Later, when I was "short" -- close enough to the end of my year-long deployment to think I might make it home -- I also found it hard to talk with the FNG's about the things we had experienced. Jerry also told me that Carl Green had suffered his third wound that day. The Brigade, Jerry said, had in response to Carl's family's complaints now instituted a policy of taking you out of the field if you had two purple hearts.

There was a second reason I knew we were lucky. While on patrol one day, our platoon passed through a small village along a riverbank. Small fishing boats were pulled up along the bank in a bit of a jumble. Suddenly, we heard a loud bang as a motor scooter backfired from about fifty feet away. Sergeant Unger leaped into a prone position in one of the boats.

"It's just a scooter backfiring," someone said.

Unger warily rose up, scanning the area carefully. Jerry Morehouse explained to me that Unger was "short," and recently had been wounded. The man behind him on a patrol had triggered a booby trap and some of that guy's foot bones had punctured Unger's buttock.

Then, a few days before May 19th, Lieutenant Walker rotated back to company headquarters in the rear to serve as Executive Officer, the "XO," which was a relatively safe job in which he would administer the paperwork and logistics of the company. He flashed us a peace sign as he boarded the Chinook helicopter taking him back. His replacement was Lieutenant Pace.

Pace gathered us in front of him and introduced himself by telling us he was a proud lifer, planning to put in twenty years. He was from Springfield, Missouri, he said, and had "twenty hours of hand- to- hand combat training and eighteen years of street-fighting experience." He was average height and weight, with thin lips not used to smiling and the kind of pinched visage I associated with the hillbillies that were sprinkled among my Central Virginia family. He wore a ridiculously large knife strapped on his belt. Through the grapevine (the company clerk back at Long Binh) we learned what was immediately obvious: Lieutenant Pace had come to this posting straight from the States and had no combat experience. The clerk also let us know Pace had "flown a desk" as an enlisted man on a previous tour, and was an OCS graduate.

For those first few days, my interactions with Lieutenant Pace were limited, as all we did was go on night ambush. Pace was quiet, speaking only to tell us when to stop and set up for the ambush. During the day, I was separate from him as he slept in the officer's area in Chris, our little Fire Support Base. But a few days after Pace took command, we were sent on a mission that threw him and me closer together: Our Company was told to get our packs and prepare for a days-long mission. We were going to an area to the west of Chris known as "The Pineapple." It was an area that had been a huge pineapple plantation during the French Colonial period and was now abandoned. Canals laced the area, and there was more Nipa-palm-and-bamboo jungle and fewer rice paddies than around Chris. From the way the older platoon members talked, it was also thick with Viet Cong.

After getting our gear together, we were trucked an hour or so to this wilder-looking part of the delta. We then struck out, walking in line, on what became an overnight march.

This is when I began doubt that Lieutenant Pace would ever be the leader I had hoped for: someone like Lieutenant Walker, or even like our Captain. I knew Captain Goodwin mostly from the radio chatter I heard as he talked with Battalion. The Colonel who ran the Battalion was frequently berating Captain Goodwin for our slow pace when on patrol. Captain Goodwin would tell the Colonel we would pick up the pace -- then, off-radio, he would tell us to go as slow as we needed to make sure we saw booby traps and potential ambushes.

"Driskill, give me the handset!" Pace would say frequently during the night of May 19th, as we pushed through stubby brush and shellhole-pocked terrain, moving along a small canal. He would then berate the lead squad for not moving fast enough. Perhaps, I thought, he was just nervous.

At some point, the whip antenna on my radio, which extended a few feet over my head, got caught in a tree branch. As I shook my body to get it free, ants fell from the tree onto me. They were stinging ants, and soon I was frantically slipping off my pack-radio included-and swatting my head and arms as the bites accumulated. I saw a water-filled shell hole nearby, and jumped in. This finally got them off me.

33

Scratching the burning bites, I saddled up again and pushed up the column to rejoin Pace. He snapped at me not to fall behind again. I tried to explain what had happened.

"Listen," he said, "I don't want excuses. Just stay up!"

Again, I thought, perhaps he's just nervous. I certainly would have been in his shoes: a brand-new leader with no combat experience leading a group of veterans with lots of on-the-job-training. I hoped he would become more like Lieutenant Walker and our captain as he gained confidence.

But that following morning, when he broke the inviolate number one rule of the Army -- Never volunteer! -- my doubts about how our mutual experience would unfold were confirmed.

After the Captain gave Pace the go-ahead, he chose a squad to go, and we saddled up in our combat gear: steel pot (helmet), ten or so 18-round ammo clips for our M16's, grenades, extra 100-round belts of M60 ammunition distributed among the squad-members, some C4 plastic explosive, and a canteen of water. As a Lieutenant, Pace carried only his own rifle and ammo and a canteen. Mike Fields, a skinny Italian-American from Cleveland, Ohio, walked point. Two riflemen followed in line, followed by Lieutenant Pace and myself, and then the rest of the squad. We also had a new "shake-and-bake" sergeant named Larry Lewis who had joined us recently. From the few hours we had been able to observe him that morning, he seemed, like Pace, anxious to get into the war.

We crossed through a patch of Nipa palm into the adjacent paddy, and Fields headed down a dike towards a scruffy little piece of growth where the Viet Cong had been spotted, our column trailing behind. Pace had instructed Fields to move along the dike, as going through the paddy would have been too slow.

Fields suddenly stopped. "Sir, I see a booby trap!"

Lieutenant Pace and I pushed up along the dike past the two riflemen, joining Fields.

"Here," he said, pointing to a thin, clear monofilament line stretching across the dike about three or four inches high. On the right side, the line disappeared into some dead grass which partially concealed a missile-shaped projectile of grey metal about 9 inches long and a few inches in diameter.

"Sir," Fields said, it looks like an unexploded twenty-millimeter cannon round."

Pace walked up close to the round, took off his helmet, and put it and his rifle on the path along that ran along the dike. He crouched down and peered at the monofilament line and the unexploded cannon round.

"I'm going to take this back and show the Captain," he said.

No! I said to myself. Even an FNG like me knew that standard operating procedure was to set up some C4 explosive and blow the booby-trap in place. Fields and the other two riflemen edged farther away down the dike. Being the RTO, I had no choice but to remain, just a yard away from Pace.

Still crouching and surveying the booby trap, Pace took out a pack of cigarettes, shook one loose and put it between his lips. After pulling out his Zippo and lighting the cigarette, he tossed the lighter and cigarette pack into his upturned steel pot by his side. He took a few long drags, then mashed the butt out in the ground. He pulled his large hunting knife out of the scabbard on his belt, and used the point to slowly pull the dead grass away from the 20-millimeter round. With the grass pulled away, we could see a handle-like jury-rigged triggering device: if the monofilament were pulled away, the handle would flip up and set off what looked like a blasting cap embedded in the round. Pace sheathed his knife, then carefully grasped the cone-shaped round, holding the handle down tight. Then he began wrapping the line around the round, which kept the handle tight and incapable of setting off the blasting cap. He carefully placed it on the ground next to his upturned helmet.

At that moment, Fields, now about forty feet further along the dike called: "Sir, another booby trap!"

Pace stood up quickly and started down the dike. After a few strides, he turned his head back to me and called out to me.

"Driskill! Get my rifle and helmet....and my cigarettes. We'll get the booby trap on the way back."

As Pace pushed beyond the two riflemen on the dike toward Fields, I dutifully bent over and grabbed Lieutenant Pace's rifle, his helmet, and his pack of cigarettes. I slung my M16 over my left shoulder and his over my right, and held his helmet in my right hand. Along with my own gear -- my rifle, my ammunition, a few grenades, and twenty-five pounds of radio and a spare battery -- I now carried Lieutenant Pace's helmet and rifle. I headed down the dike towards the new booby trap.

I took three, maybe four steps, when a rushing wall of explosive sound seemed to roll up my right leg, and I felt myself thrown straight up into the air. The fourth man down the trail, I had tripped a booby trap.

The next thing I realized was that I was coming down in what seemed like a head-first position into the side of a dike. A black fog seemed to blur my vision, and I felt I was passing out. My legs felt numb, as if they had fallen asleep. Then a sudden rush of pain through my legs took away the numbness and brought me back to full awareness: it felt how I thought it would feel if someone were beating my legs with baseball bats.

My ears were ringing, but I began to clear the fog from my head. Pace was kneeling at my feet, and had his ridiculously large knife out, slicing my boot off of my right foot. Blood was soaking through my pants legs, slowly spreading. My right foot was not identifiable as a foot: it looked like bloody steak. And my legs continued to feel as if someone were alternately pounding them with baseball bats and then crushing them.

Someone was applying bandages to my foot and ripping my pants legs to get to the legs underneath. Pace looked worried but was saying, "Don't worry, you'll be back carrying my radio soon."

But Morehead Sam was crouched by my head, and told me "Hey, your war is over. You're going home with this one."

I must have slipped out of consciousness, because the next thing I remember was lying in the dust off chopper, continuously yelling "Fuck! Fuck! Fuck!" while rice paddies slipped by beneath us. We landed at what I learned was Third Field Hospital in Saigon, an old colonial building in the midst of the crowded city, and a couple of enlisted men pulled me out of the chopper and onto a rolling stretcher. They took me into a room, and other people began getting the rest of my clothes off. A doctor was peering at my wounds, which were on both legs, my right arm, and the right side of my head. The flak jacket must have done its job of protecting my torso.

Soon they moved me to another room. My legs still felt like they were being pounded and crushed, I could not feel my right foot, and I continued to say "Fuck! Fuck! Fuck!" A woman doctor with a French accent entered and explained they were going to use local anesthetic and remove the shrapnel.

"Watch your language, soldier!" ordered a sergeant from somewhere behind me.

I shut up: Army training, I guess. Or maybe it was just due to my upbringing, which inculcated in me a deference to authority. But I thought, I'm in real pain here, why can't I curse?

As the doctor snipped away at my flesh, stopping to pull out the metal fragments, I occasionally told her I was feeling her cutting. She matter-of-factly injected some more Novocain, then continued. As I was learning, even when one is wounded the Army provides no frills.

At some point, the doctor was finished, my legs were wrapped in gauze from toes to hips, and I was wheeled to a ward which was to be my home for the next nine days.

The first few days passed in a haze, though I was acutely aware of a deep ache in my legs. A colonel came through and pinned a purple heart on my pillowcase. A doctor came through each morning and looked at my wounds and had them re-bandaged. About the fifth day, they put me in a wheel chair and took me to a club of sorts on the premises, where a Vietnamese band played Motown and Country music. I began to feel better, but had not done more than get out of the bed – gingerly -- and into the wheelchair.

I hoped I was eventually on my way back to the United States. With the pain in my legs and the ugly-looking wounds to my right foot, I thought they were simply waiting for me to improve enough to handle the long flight home. I wrote my parents to tell them what had happened, and what I thought was going to happen.

The American National Red Cross

Dear Folks,

As you can probably tell by the stationary I'm using, I've changed addresses since my last letter. Don't worry, though, I'm all in one piece and will be as good as new in a few months. It's really an excellent wound -- we call it the million-dollar wound over here -- because it leaves no permanent damage and will keep me out of the field for a good 4 to 6 months -- maybe even permanently if they've got a spot in the rear when I'm well. You know the old saying -- you find some of them all the time, some of them some of the time, but never all of them all of the time. Well, that's the way I was with a certain booby trap I happened to trip yesterday. I've got some holes in my arms and legs, but nothing serious -- it just takes time to heal. As you can tell, I'm not feeling bad at all -- it's been less than twenty-four hours since I was hit. As soon as the wound stabilizes they'll probably send me to Japan. Since I don't have any broken bones, I probably won't go home, but you can never tell. I might get lucky. I reiterate that there is no cause for alarm -- I'm fine, and as a matter of fact, rather lucky in being out of the field. I'm sending youall my purple heart also --nothing like a medal to pin on my mighty chest, huh? I won't send an address, as I don't know it, and it will probably change shortly. If it looks like I will be here awhile, I'll write you my address. Anything you must write me will reach me through my old address. That's about it from this end.

Bob

PS I was going to send you my purple heart but have lost it already. Maybe next time.

This was not to be the last time I would be wrong about my war being over. The eighth day, they stitched up my wounds (which had been left open initially to heal from the inside out). The morning of the ninth day, an orderly came in and read to the ward the orders regarding who was to be transported where for the next stage of our recoveries. I would be going to the 6th Convalescent Center at Cam Rhan Bay, I was told.

A convalescent center? This didn't sound like I was on my way home.

"Get up." The orderly stood by my bed. "Let's go, the bus is waiting."

Get up? On my feet?

"I can't get up! I can't get out of bed!"

He looked again at the orders he was holding. "Nope. Driskill. Ambulatory. Cam Rhan Bay."

Ambulatory? I tried to get out of the bed and stand up. My legs screamed in protest. I managed to stand, but could not for the life of me imagine taking a step.

The orderly watched me for a moment, then went out for a bit, and came back with a cane.

"Use this. But I checked: the doctors say you are ambulatory."

Surely this is a mistake, I thought. But I gamely shuffled out of the ward with the others who were going to Cam Rhan Bay. They trucked us to an airfield, and I shuffled up the big ramp that extended from the back of a cargo plane. We were told to sit in webbed seats along the sides, and off we went. I could not wait to get to the hospital in Cam Rhan Bay and get this misunderstanding about my supposed ambulatory status cleared up.

After leaving the plane for another bus, we moved through a large bustling complex -- an air base, I would learn -- into a separate fenced-in area with dozens of identical barracks-like buildings. These were our wards. As usual in the army, they were arranged in two rows facing a main "street" that was nothing more than boards on top of sand. At the head of the street stood what appeared to be a headquarters building and a mess hall. The back of one row faced a long stretch of sand extending to the South China Sea.

An E4 – the pay grade between a Private First Class and a Sergeant -- gathered a group of us and led us to a ward -- a long open space lined with cots, with screening between a chest-high wall and the start of the roof. He told us to wait there for a doctor to see us. Leaning my cane against the wall behind me, I gratefully collapsed on my cot, eagerly anticipating a reversal of my "ambulatory" status.

Shortly, a doctor -- a Major by rank -- and his small coterie of aids entered the ward and began moving from cot to cot, reading each patient's medical history and explaining, I assumed, what treatment each patient required. When he reached my cot, he scanned my records.

"Shrapnel wounds in your legs and arm and head," he said. "Nine days ago. You were exceptionally lucky: all that shrapnel and no broken bones. No major arteries hit. Quite remarkable."

"Yes sir," I replied. "They seem to have made a mistake at Third Field, though. They have me listed as ambulatory."

The Major looked at my records again.

"No," he said, "no mistake." He told one of his entourage to unwrap the gauze that encased my legs from toes to hip, and to take off the bandage on my upper arm. He peered at the collection of stitched wounds. "We'll take out the stitches in a few days. Until then, keep the wounds open, and make sure to swim in the ocean." Noticing my cane, he leaned over and grabbed it.

"You won't be needing this, either."

I was stunned. True, the trip from Third Field had shown me that I could walk, but with real pain (although, to be honest, the pain had diminished the more I had walked). But this was my treatment: swim in the ocean -- and if you want to eat, walk to the mess hall?

After the doctor left the building, we new arrivals began getting to know each other and the inhabitants who had preceded us. It turned out that we were all under the same treatment plan: swim, and walk everywhere you wanted to go. The veterans, as it were, told us our only responsibility would be to make our cots up each day. They also explained our presence in the ward: If your wounds were expected to heal, they said, allowing you to rejoin your unit within sixty days, you were sent here. If longer than sixty but less than ninety, you were sent to Japan. Longer than ninety days and you were sent "back to the World," which is what we called going home.

So for the next fifty days, Cam Rhan Bay was my home. As my legs healed, I began to think of this as the best Army duty I'd ever had: make your cot, go to chow, spend the day swimming in the ocean and hanging out with buddies. I got to know lots of guys, as well as how the war was proceeding in other areas. The battle of Hamburger Hill was being fought then, and many casualties from the 101st airborne were at Cam Rhan Bay. One of my buddies from AIT was there. An FNG, he had been walking point in the A Shaw valley when an ambush led to bullet wounds in his lower legs. His war was fought in thick jungle, a far different experience from mine in the Delta.

I met two marines, as well. Wounded marines usually were attended to by the Navy on hospital ships, but May of 1969 had filled all of those beds up. Their war was also in jungle. They called being in the Marines being in "the Crotch," and complained that their officers refused re-supply sometimes because it made their unit seem "soft."

My closest friend was Tony Ferragamo, a fellow Baltimorean from the 9th Division. The 9th fought in the Delta, like the 199th. He had shrapnel in his back from a firefight in which his column of APC's were ambushed. The Colonel who had come by in the Third Field in Saigon had congratulated him on the fine job his unit had done and told him there had been something like a few dozen enemy KIA's. Tony worked the machine gun on one of the APC's and told me that sure, they might have killed a couple of VC, but they suffered a lot of casualties themselves.

We were learning: somewhere along the chain of command, the reports from the field of how many enemy we had killed were being inflated.

About halfway through my stay, as I walked down the road between the barracks, an entire squad from my old platoon appeared, walking towards me. Mike Gross, Ken Handy, a kid from Michigan named Fred Derry, and a few others, broke into smiles as we approached

"Driskill!" Mike said. "How are you doing?"

I briefly thought they had somehow arranged a visit: they had no visible injuries.

"What are you guys doing here?"

"Hey, we were all riding an APC when it hit a mine. We were blown off. They sent us here from Third Field. They'll probably send us back in a few days."

So for a few days, we all swam and lazed about. Ken Handy, though, had back pain from the incident that grew worse each day. Eventually he was sent to Japan. Fred Derry, who had befriended me immediately when I joined the platoon because I had spent a year in Michigan, kept talking about re-enlisting and getting out of the field. Re-enlisting meant signing on for another, brand-new, three-year hitch. The enticement was that you would be guaranteed a new Military Occupation Specialty, one that was NOT infantry.

"It's three more years, I know, but this is a wake-up call for me. There's a lot of danger out in the field."

Fred was the first, but not the last, to come the conclusion that an extra couple of years in the Army doing some relatively safe job was preferable to hoping you would beat the lottery of the infantry. He re-upped, and I never saw him again.

When the staff started making Mike Gross fill sandbags during the day, he told them he was ready to go back to the field.

The time for me to rejoin my company eventually arrived. My mother wrote me that she could not believe someone would be sent back into combat once he had been wounded. I patiently explained that the policy in the 199th -- throughout Vietnam, for all I knew -- was that you would be removed from the field if you were wounded twice, not once.

When I rejoined the company, it had been moved from the Delta into an area northeast of Saigon that was covered with triple-canopy jungle interspersed with rubber and coffee plantations. The Brigade had a new commander, "Body-Count Bennett," who, according to rumor, had volunteered us for this new Area of Operation in hopes of getting his second star. There were no booby traps to worry about, but we were told we would be engaged in more firefights. The guys told me they had not yet had any enemy contact. It would be a different kind of combat.

Chapter Four

The Jungle

The first jungle firefight
   I was no longer an FNG and so quietly declined Lieutenant Pace's offer for me to carry his radio again. I was happy to be just a rifleman in one of our three squads, and I was assigned to what I remember as "Gallion's squad." Squads had numbers, but we all referred to them by the leader's last name. Gallion -- I don't remember his first name, if I ever knew it -- was our squad leader. Short, with curly blond hair, he had a potbelly that he claimed had always been a part of his physique. He came from a tiny Ozark Mountain town, a town so small he had never met a black person before he was drafted. He was cheerful, as well as earnest about doing a good job as squad leader. He wanted to be fair in terms of distributing the dangers we faced, and to keep us safe while still getting the job done.
   Stinger, who had come to the company with me in April, was still with us. Curtis Dewitt had joined the platoon just before I was wounded. He was a tall, bony South Carolina farm boy. The rest of the squad was made up of new guys -- new to me, at least.
   Richard "Dicky" Dixon was, like Gallion, a short guy, maybe five feet six inches, with curly blond hair. But he was from the big city: Los Angeles. Before being drafted, he had boxed some Golden Gloves and had spent some time in a juvenile jail. He had an unfailingly sunny disposition, never letting the daily frustrations of life in the field get him down. He was married and had a daughter whose picture he carried. Jesse Rabenda was a blond kid from Chicago who never stopped extolling the virtues of being from Chicago. And Jackson -- again, I can't remember, or maybe never knew, his first name -- was a black farm boy from South Carolina who had never been to a town or city until he was a teenager. Finally, Lloyd Cook, a wiry black guy from New Orleans who had been a porter in the merchant marine until drafted, took over the M60 from Stinger.
   The squad was like a small, intimate family. We were always together when on the move or on a squad-size ambush; we set up in adjacent three-man positions at night; and we shared a bunker when back at the artillery outpost we thought of as our "base."
   In the rest of the platoon were other new-to me-faces. James Clarkson was the unfortunate FNG who had gotten the job of Pace's RTO. He was an only child from a family in the little Northwest Georgia town of Trion. Like Dicky Dixon, he was never dispirited for any appreciable time. I picture his face even now as always in a smile.

41

New in Michael Gross's squad were "Tiny" Glinka -- who of course was big, maybe six feet three inches tall -- Peterson, Jensen, and Dan Weirich. Tiny had left a brand-new wife back in the World and talked about her incessantly. Petersen had been raised Mormon, but he drank and smoked and claimed not to believe in Mormonism any more. He told us that people like him were known among Mormons as Jack Mormons. Despite his outward disdain for the religion of his upbringing, he was very close to Jensen, a stocky blond still-devout Mormon. I remember Jensen as never joining in with the rest of us in our relentless complaining about the heat, the bugs, the mud, the officers, and anything and everything else associated with our life in the Army: he was the platoon stoic. He carried the M79 grenade launcher for Gross's squad. The grenade launcher was a shotgun-like weapon that fired either a grenade for longer-range shots or a shotgun round for shorter ones. Dan Weirich was a quiet guy who had been drafted after completing college. His father had been a newspaper reporter, and Dan hoped to follow in his footsteps when he returned to civilian life.

Finally, new to the third squad -- called "Graham's squad", because Graham, another South Carolina farm boy, was the leader -- was Martin Clay. Clay was from the small town of Redkey, Indiana. He talked longingly of his small-town life that he obviously missed immensely. Everyone knew everyone back in Redkey, and life was seemingly uncomplicated by the yearning for excitement.

And we had a new platoon medic, Doc Clary. Doc was a tall, thin guy, pretty much just out of high school, who wore wire rim glasses. He had what my family called "Black Irish" features: very black hair and eyelashes, and dark eyes.

Doc was also a conscientious objector. He had the aura -- and, it turned out, the substance -- of an intellectual, even though he had not yet attended college. Perhaps this was because he was the medic, who had specialized knowledge. Perhaps it was because he was from Northern California.

Even though by rights Doc should have marched and bivouacked with Lieutenant Pace and his RTO, he spent as much time with our squad as possible. No one seemed to want to spend time with Pace. But Doc couldn't avoid bivouacking with Pace all of the time, and was thus a source of insight about the man -- both then, and later.

None of these new guys had experienced any combat yet. To my mind, they seemed far too casual and sanguine about what I knew to be the dangerous environment in which we lived. They would ask me, "What's it like to be hit?" and I somehow failed to convey how much it could hurt and how small was the margin between a bad wound and a disabling or fatal one.

But I found Doc to have the imagination necessary to appreciate our danger. Perhaps this was aided by his having almost daily to pull another piece of shrapnel out as it worked its way through my skin. Or perhaps it was his intellectualism; it turned out that Doc was better read than even the college boys in the platoon. Whatever the reason, he seemed fully aware of the dangers that awaited us.

Pace, unfortunately, was still with us. I wondered whether he was just as hungry as he had been when I met him to win fame and glory by leading us in combat.

The answer, I was soon told, was yes.   To a man, the platoon told me Pace was unremittingly gung ho. He was also universally disliked: he was sour, surly, and unwilling or unable to take an interest in the lives of his troops. To make matters worse, the few reports we got from his new RTO, the unfortunate Clarkson, were that in the presence of the company captain (now a West Pointer, Captain Rantalla), he would talk about how he wished his platoon was tougher, and how it needed some enemy contact to keep it on its toes.

And, unbelievably, he was sloppy about his weapon: his M16 had rust on its barrel and what looked like gummy mud paste around the working parts. He was never seen cleaning either his rifle or his ammunition. Rust on the barrel might not affect the workings of the rifle, but if Basic had taught us anything, it was to have an attachment to your weapon almost like one you might have for an animate object like a dog. You needed almost to love it. And you didn't let something you loved get rusty and dirty.

This was dangerous for everyone, as we all would depend on one another in a fire fight, and the M16 was a delicate weapon. It didn't do well in the heat and dirt and mud of Vietnam. And it needed clean ammunition as well, which was hard to accommodate, as your eighteen-round ammo clips slid beneath you in the dirt as you crawled and clawed your way through jungle. But as hard as it was to keep rifle and ammo clean, to not at least try was to invite disaster.

Our life in these jungles and rubber and coffee plantations was a lot different than it had been in the Delta. In the Delta, most of the time we patrolled from our fort for a night or a day. At the fort, a Chinook helicopter brought us daily deliveries of ice, and cola, and even some beer: at the end of patrol, a cold drink and a cot in a bunker awaited us. And the biggest danger was booby traps.

In our new environment we did have a base of operations: Fire Base Libby, an artillery base atop a knoll stripped clean of vegetation, surrounded by a perimeter of concertina wire backed by big bunkers. The bunkers were just big rectangular holes, maybe eight by twelve feet, and four feet deep, covered with roof timbers the size of railroad ties which were then covered with sandbags. There was a two-foot gap between the roof and ground level, allowing us to enter from the back and fire out of the front. There were big rats as well, crawling along the timbers. These bunkers held six or eight men, with hammocks strung for sleeping. Our company was responsible for manning a portion of this perimeter, so our platoon intermittently lived in these bunkers for a few days at a time.   The artillery unit had cold-water showers and even outhouses, which we could use. All in all, we learned to think of our time spent at Libby as relatively safe and comfortable.

Even so, when we were at Libby we were on alert as a ready reaction force, available to move out in support of other units engaged in enemy contact, or in response to new, breaking intelligence. These quick strike reactions frequently involved hopping on helicopters and being dropped in a jungle clearing (where else in the jungle could a helicopter set down?), surrounded by a tree line in which NVA could be concealed and able to fire on us from cover.

It was on one of these quick-reaction insertions, very soon after I rejoined the platoon, that I confirmed my belief that Doc had the proper imagination for our situation. Saddled up with just our combat gear -- weapons, ammunition, and water -- we lined up on the little landing area at Libby and boarded a flight of helicopters. These "slicks," as we called them, had an open compartment that held maybe six of us, hanging on to something inside with our feet dangling outside. Loaded up with our platoon, the choppers wheeled, elevated, and took off over the jungle.

Doc and I were seated next to each other. With my heightened sense of danger, I was, very very scared. From the look on Doc's face, it appeared that he too was appropriately fearful.

Finally, we approached an open area surrounded by jungle. The machine gunners on the slick opened up on the tree line as we flared into the opening, and as the chopper hovered a few feet above ground, we jumped into about six inches of water, maybe thirty or forty yards from the tree line. We slogged through the water as fast as we could, forming a line parallel to the tree line with our rifles' selector switches on full automatic, barrels pointing forward.

No fire came from the tree line. We hit the jungle, swinging our weapons in arcs as we anticipated an enemy. But there was nothing. We moved a little farther into the jungle, still found nothing, and then were ordered to return to the clearing, where helicopters again flew in, flared a moment over the surface, and waited while we jumped on board.

I sat next to Doc flying back.

"This reminds me of a line from a poem," I shouted to him. *"Six miles from earth, loosed from its dream of life."*

I had taken introductory poetry (twice, having failed the first time) at Michigan State. On one exam, we were given a poem and asked to interpret the symbolism. This exam question was my one shining moment in the class: I alone made the symbolic connections. The poem was about a bomber mission in World War II, in which the ball turret gunner, suspended beneath the plane in a plexiglass turret which he swiveled to fire at enemy fighters, was killed. The line was from that poem. Flying into that LZ made life prior to enlistment, with baseball games and worries about whether a certain girl liked me, seem like a dream remembered.

"Yeah, 'Death of a Ball Turret Gunner,'" Doc said. "Written by Randall Jarrell."

I was impressed.

But most of our time would be spent in the jungle, packs loaded with C rations (a collection of terrible canned foods, a little toilet paper, and four cigarettes), five-gallon bladders of water, our entrenching tool, and all our combat gear: about ninety pounds of weight. And we were to spend as long as five weeks at a time out there, wearing the same uniforms, chopping our way through what seemed like impenetrable jungle, sweating profusely, stopping every hour or so to use a burning cigarette to get accumulated leaches to drop off our skin and to re-douse ourselves with mosquito repellent. So little sun penetrated the upper canopies of the jungle -- the top one maybe a hundred and fifty feet above us, sometimes a second one lower down -- that we white guys were as pale as if we worked in an office. We would get re-supplied by chopper with C rations and water -- and ammo, if needed -- every third or fourth day.

By late July the platoon had been doing this for a few weeks, and had yet to engage in a firefight. We had found evidence of Charley in the form of some weapons caches, with maybe a group of Rocket Propelled Grenade Launchers ("RPG's") and mortar rounds and even some rifles. We had even hunkered down as an air strike attacked a suspected bunker complex maybe fifty yards away, sending chunks of metal maybe the size of a hand (at least they seemed that big in memory) *thwump*ing into the trees above us. But we had not been fired upon.

Doc had been regularly taking his tweezers and pulling small metal fragments from my body -- mostly from my ankles, but some from my arms, and even my earlobe. Finally he sent me back on a resupply chopper to have my leg looked at.

I was delighted. Brigade Main Base was Shangri-La, with showers, cots, and an enlisted man's club with cold beer. I didn't think they would take me out of the field, but a day or two in the rear would be a welcome respite.

I got back to company headquarters in the late afternoon, dropped my gear off on a wonderful-looking cot, put on a fresh, clean uniform and was sent to the medical office. An orthopedic surgeon saw me, but told me to return the next morning: they were closing down for the day in a few minutes, at 17:00 hours. What excellent luck! Maybe I would get another full day in the rear. Such small pleasures loomed large in the life of a rifleman.

With an extra spring in my step, I walked back towards our company headquarters maybe half a mile away. From behind, a jeep pulled up beside me.

"Where're you heading, soldier?" the officer inside asked.

"Charley Fifth of the Twelfth."

"Hop in. I'll give you a lift."

Ah, what an exceptional officer. When you walk to war for a living with as much as 90 pounds on your back, a lift is not to be turned down. And what a pleasant change: earlier, on my way over, a Rear Echelon Mother Fucker – "REMF" -- officer had stopped me and told me to "look more like a soldier -- stop slouching, shave," and so on. He had no concept of what life in the field was like, and how little tolerance we dogfaces had for the chickenshit rear-echelon bullshit he seemed so fond of. The officer now offering me a ride had obviously seen me for the hardened field soldier I was and had appreciated me for the dangers and hardships I faced that he didn't.

As we drove, he asked me why I was here at Long Binh, and I explained about my recent injury, and how Doc had sent me back to get checked, and how the orthopod Doctor had told me to come back the next day.

He suddenly stopped, did a three-point turn, and headed back the way we had come, his mouth drawn down.

"That's not right, soldier. We're here to support you men out in the field. There's no reason the orthopedic clinic can't see you tonight." He turned towards me a little, and a slight, small smile creased his face. "I'm the commander of this medical unit. We're going to have you looked at now."

Nooooo! I said to myself. But back we headed. At the orthopedic building, he accompanied me in and explained to the doctor -- still there, but obviously headed out, probably to a pleasant night of drinking at the Officers Club -- that I was to be seen immediately. The orthopod was clearly not happy at the interruption, and perhaps more unhappy at the clear, if restrained, upbraiding by the commander.

Seen I was. Poked, prodded, and x-rayed by an irritated doctor, I had little hope now of being sent to a rear job. And I was not mistaken.

"The x-ray shows an old fracture in your smaller lower-leg bone," I was told. "Perhaps you shouldn't have been sent back to the field so soon, but it's fully healed now. You have metal fragments, but none big enough to require removal-they should have done a better job at the beginning. But you're fit for duty."

So the next morning I was put on a truck and that afternoon I rejoined my Platoon at Libby. I found I had missed their first firefight. Through an adrenaline high, Dixon, Rabenda, Stinger, and the rest of the platoon filled me in.

That morning, the platoon had been the ready reaction force. Bravo Company had reported making contact with an NVA force, and our platoon was trucked to a spot and told to move through the jungle on a compass heading toward Bravo. The plan, it appeared, was to hope the NVA moved away from Bravo towards us, whereupon we would engage them.

Our three squads moved out in single file, with first squad leading the way. Pace, almost twitching with anticipation, I was told, was up with the first squad leader, Mike Gross. Our squad was second in line, and Sergeant Lewis was in line right behind our squad leader, Gallion. The third squad brought up the rear.

After about a half hour of chopping through the jungle, Clark Ferrell, the point man, came across a less dense patch. A few steps into this little area, he came across something that looked like a cabana at the beach: a small building cloaked in vegetation, maybe banana-tree leaves. Peering more closely, he realized that this was, in the vernacular, a "shitter." A path wandered on through the jungle from this little latrine. The platoon, Ferrell realized, had come upon the outskirts of an NVA or VC base camp.

Back in the middle of the column, my squad heard about all of this as each man relayed in whispers what was going on. At some point the squad heard the whispered report that Pace was going to walk point down the trail.

This, of course, was not standard operating procedure. The Lieutenant is the nerve center of the platoon. While certainly there are risks he should take, walking point was not one of them. If it turned out to be a base camp, he would be needed to make decisions: Call in artillery? An air strike? Send a squad in a flanking movement?

But concerns about the wisdom of Pace walking point were, it turned out, unwarranted. What actually happened was that Pace simply moved forward to join Ferrell and Mike Gross as they entered the base camp.

Consisting of a series of bunkers, the base camp was deserted, though NVA backpacks were lined up neatly atop the bunkers, awaiting their owners' return. The NVA from the camp were apparently engaged with Bravo on the far side of the camp. (Intelligence, for once, had got some facts right.)

Gross turned around as he heard Pace approach, surprised that he had come forward instead of waiting back in the column for a report. Turning back to face the base camp, he saw NVA approaching. Reflexively, Gross pointed his M16 and emptied a full clip -- eighteen rounds -- at the approaching enemy. One appeared to die on the spot, and another was hit in the legs but managed to get inside a bunker, from which he began returning fire. Ferrell found cover somewhere, and Gross jumped behind a large tree trunk, pinned down now by AK-47 fire coming from the bunker. Scanning the area, he realized Pace was nowhere to be seen.

Back in the column where my squad was, the ripping sound of automatic weapons fire, with overhanging twigs and branches getting clipped off, told the squad that the platoon was being fired upon.

Pressed as close to the ground as possible, they awaited orders. But nothing came over the radio. No directions for the rest of the platoon. Sergeant Lewis tried to raise Pace but got no response.

Sporadic "zings" as bullets flew overhead and to either side of the squad kept them prone, except for Lewis, crouching next to the RTO. Lewis paused for a moment after failing to raise Pace.

"I'm taking third squad around to the left and see if we can flank them, he said to my squad. "We'll move fast. Stay put for now."

So the squad hugged the ground as sporadic fire continued to pass overhead. The occasional M16 burst seemed to respond to the AK fire. The squad waited, still prone; the high-velocity whine of rounds going by and the thought of what they could do to a body kept everyone truly hugging the ground. After a few minutes, there was a loud explosion, then no more automatic weapons fire.

"Cease fire, cease fire, area secure!" Lewis, on the third squad radio, was yelling. "Two gook Kilo India Alpha's!"

The squad slowly crawled forward, passing a big log across the trail, and then arriving at a small bunker complex. Pace and Lewis were standing by the first bunker, a rectangle dug in the ground, about four by eight feet. It had a log roof covered with a foot of dirt, raised about a foot above ground, which left a firing position facing the trail. Lewis was giving directions for the platoon to fan out in a perimeter.

Pace got on the radio and reported to Battalion that we had two confirmed kills, with no casualties for ourselves. After a little while, first squad collected the NVA knapsacks -- some full of documents, we were later told -- and then was tasked with blowing up with C4 the four bunkers that made up the complex while the other squads maintained the perimeter. When that was done, orders came down from Battalion and the platoon formed up in column and headed back out towards the initial drop-off point.

Going past the now-destroyed bunker complex, everyone looked at the two dead NVA. Each of their heads had been partially shorn off by a grenade Lewis had lobbed into the bunker. For most, it was the first dead body they had seen. Adrenaline was still high, though, and there was little philosophical contemplation about the death of other humans. This would change as we saw more dead bodies, though.

Reaching the road at the initial point of entry to the jungle, the platoon got picked up by trucks and was taken back to Libby.

And it was back at Libby, where I had just arrived, that first squad filled the rest of the platoon on what had happened up front. As Clarkson related it: "Man, when they opened up, Pace dropped like a rock, then low-crawled back and got behind this fallen log. Mike was left up close to where the firing was coming from, standing behind a tree. I crawled up to Pace behind his log. He raised up to fire his rifle over top of the log, and.... click! Nothing, it didn't fire! So he reaches over and grabs mine! But he didn't fire it. He just stayed down behind the log. I can hear Mike firing some bursts. Before I got behind the log, I saw an AK firing out of a bunker. How they fucking missed Pace, I don't know."

Third platoon then told us how they had come up behind the bunker, saw some movement in it, and then Lewis lobbed a grenade into it. The AK firing stopped. Lewis crawled up, looked in, and said: "Two KIA, that's all. Check the other bunkers."

And it was over. Our platoon had been shot at, and everyone agreed it was the scariest thing that had ever happened in their lives.

It made a difference for everyone. Some of the platoon had been curious. What would it be like to be fired upon? Would they freeze, or do their jobs? Before the fight, some had been bored, and thought combat would break the tedium of spending our days sweating our way through the jungle. Now it seemed as if all of us would be happy to never have another firefight.

Even Sergeant Lewis felt this way. After the fight, as we stopped one day for a break from pushing through the jungle, Ferrell, who had a college degree and seemed to me older, wiser, and cynical, asked Lewis: "Are you still gung ho?"

"Nope," Lewis said. He then paused a moment, and explained. "I'll admit, I was when I got here -- I wanted to see what combat would be like. But I'll be happy if we never have contact again."

It turned out this firefight was the watershed event for Lieutenant Pace, and it had repercussions for us for months to come, until Pace left the field. We heard reports that he would still tell the Captain about how "a little contact keeps the platoon sharp," and acted hard and tough in front of him. But we lived and fought with the man, and came to know better: he had developed a singular focus on his own survival that would endanger the rest of us.

But first, a few weeks later, the Battalion Commander met our platoon out at Libby for a ceremony in which Lieutenant Pace and Mike Gross were both given the Army Commendation Medal with the "V" device for valor: a medal for bravery. We grumbled about this a little. Mike deserved it, he had moved up and returned fire with no one supporting him, but why did Pace get one? We assumed it was a quid pro quo: Mike got one only if Pace got one. Or was simply walking up to the front of the column cause for a medal? If that was so, every man who walked point would deserve one sooner or later.

Doc's lonely crawl

Our routine continued: moved by truck or helicopter to some point, the platoon was given a compass heading and told to follow it. Often, thick vines and brush required us to either zigzag around it, looking for an opening, or to cut through it with a machete. Using the machete made a racket, creating a ringing noise as the blade made partial cuts in the thick hardwood of the vines. When we moved like this, the enemy could surely hear us coming.

The platoon moved in single file, with a rifleman on each side of the column about thirty or forty feet away, depending on the thickness of the jungle. (These "flankers" had to maintain visual contact with the column.) Squads were rotated day by day between being first in line, in the middle, or bringing up the rear.

Every few hundred yards, the column would stop and the leading squad would make a circular patrol to one side of the line of march, while the trailing squad did one to the left. These "cloverleaf" circles had a diameter of a few hundred yards. In this way, we effectively searched a swath of jungle about five hundred yards wide as we moved along our compass heading. While the cloverleafs were being carried out, the remaining squad formed a small perimeter around the Lieutenant and his RTO and the medic.

Early one afternoon, roughly three weeks after our first firefight, we stopped in a small clearing surrounded by thick jungle, and our squad and Mike Gross's squad set out on our cloverleafs. By now, I always walked point for our squad: I had a knack for zigzagging around jungle brush while still keeping us on our compass heading. This meant we could move quietly. And I did not trust some FNG to be quiet and observant, which were the key qualities a point man should have. For new guys, what seemed like the sheer implausibility of having to move through impenetrable brush while carrying 90 pounds sapped their will to try and move quietly.

We had gone maybe fifty yards away from where Graham's squad had formed their perimeter around Pace. Then, from about where Gross's squad should have been by that time, large explosive booms and the crackling sound of AK's as well as the deeper rolling sound of heavy machine gun fire ripped through the afternoon stillness.

Our squad immediately flattened out on the ground and looked through the underbrush towards where the firing was coming from. A single round zipped directly over my head -- maybe a foot above, maybe just a few inches -- and I frantically inched back a yard or so into a slight depression in the ground, looking to get as flat and low as possible. I actually kicked Rabenda in his head to make him make room for me. The realization that the round would have gone through my head if it had been a little lower or if I had been a little higher had momentarily frightened me to the extent that all I could think about was getting closer to the ground. It reminded me of a World War II cartoon by Bill Mauldin that I had seen as a child in a book on my parents' bookshelf: as tracer rounds are depicted flying overhead, one infantryman says to another, "I can't get any lower, me buttons are in the way."

No more rounds came at us, even though the sound of AK's and M16's and claymores and machine-gun fire continued.

"I think it was just a round that got through the brush when it missed somebody," Rabenda said.

"Driskill, you see anything out there?" Gallion asked.

I said no, and the squad quickly agreed that no one had us in their sights. It was just a bullet that had made it through the brush after missing a target closer to the shooter.

We heard another explosion, then heard Mike Gross on the radio: "Taking automatic weapons fire and claymores from bunkers, we have one Whiskey India Alpha."

We heard nothing in response from Lieutenant Pace. Then the radio crackled again and we heard Pace telling Gallion to bring our squad back to him. Gallion scowled.

49

"You heard him, head back," he told me. I think we all wanted to move toward the sound of the fight, not back to Pace. But we retraced our steps, and very carefully entered the perimeter set up by Graham's squad. Pace instructed Cook to set up with his machine gun facing the sound of the firefight. Graham's squad already had their M60 trained in the same direction.

The picture was this: Pace was crouched along with his RTO inside a tight perimeter with two machine guns covering any approach from the direction of the firefight. There was no sign of Lewis, or of Doc. Gallion asked the Lieutenant if he should move our squad up to the fight. Pace shook his head. We then filled in the openings in the perimeter between Graham's men.

Minutes went by, with automatic weapons clattering away from where Gross's squad was. Why, I wondered, was Pace not sending us forward? Why did he not have our two biggest guns, the M60's, up in the fight? The first rule when in a firefight, we had been told, was get the 60's up. That's why FNG's got to carry them, after all: it's dangerous duty because the guns go to the fight.

After a few more minutes, the sounds of AK's and the heavy machine gun became sparse and intermittent while the sounds of M16's grew more prevalent. Then all firing petered out, and Sergeant Lewis came up on the radio, saying we had two confirmed NVA KIA's and a blood trail.

The fight was over. But we knew we had our own wounded, and someone from Gross's squad came back and told us Ferrell had a sucking chest wound. We needed a medivac.

Unlike in the movies, medivacs as a rule would not land unless we had secured a landing zone. To do this, our squad was sent to circle our little clearing to make sure the enemy was gone. When we had finished the patrol, we sent the all-clear by radio to Pace. We saw smoke popped -- a colored smoke grenade set off to identify the landing zone -- and heard the medivac approach, land, and take off. When we returned to the little clearing, Doc was there, looking somewhat agitated, and told us both Ferrell and Mike Gross had been choppered out. Mike, Doc said, had some scratches on his arm from claymore shrapnel. This would be his second purple heart, and would get him out of the field. Ferrell, Doc said, had been shot, with the bullet entering up by his neck and exiting around his waist.

Pace was on the radio, sounding like he was talking to Battalion Command. After signing off, he told us a dog unit was being choppered in to follow the blood trail.

In a few minutes, a chopper arrived, hovered a few feet off the ground, and let off two handlers and their dog. Pace assigned our squad to go with them, and we headed down the trail Ferrell had made to the bunker complex.

The complex was big: maybe ten bunkers. At the base of one of them, two dead NVA were slumped against its wall. Sergeant Lewis called us over and pointed out a blood trail leading out into the jungle. The dog handlers gave their Labrador a sniff and off we went following the trail, with the dog in the lead, the handlers close behind holding the leash, and then me, followed by our squad.

We moved methodically, the dog sniffing and moving, sniffing again, and then moving a few feet before repeating the performance. We could see patches of blood as we went. The handlers seemed hyper-alert. One of them explained that they did this all the time and it worked on their nerves: you're always heading to where you know the enemy has just been, and even if wounded, could be lying in wait.

We stopped by as small stream.

"Look," the lead dog handler told us, "we probably can't pick up the trail on the other side, and this looks like a good spot for the gooks to set up an ambush. Let's recon by fire and return."

So the squad crept up and spread out in the brush on the bank of the stream, and each of us fired a clip into the far bank. We got no return fire. We turned around and headed back.

Back at the NVA base camp we were ordered to saddle up, and the platoon set out on a new compass heading. After maybe an hour, the sun was setting as we came upon the beginnings of a new base camp. A small clearing had been created where trees had been felled and cut into lengths that could serve as bunker roofs. Fresh partially-dug rectangular holes were spread out in a perimeter. Pace announced we would set up here for the night.

I was dumbfounded. Setting up for the night in a location that had to be known to the NVA? It was their new base camp, after all. They could mortar us, or attack us at night. Maybe we were going to move once more after dark?

But Pace had no such plans. This was to be our night defensive position. To put us more on edge, Graham's squad did a patrol outside the perimeter and brought back an NVA claymore -- theirs were disks, about four inches thick and a foot in diameter that we called "Chicom Claymores" because they were supplied by the Chinese Communists -- that had been pointed towards us. It appeared that the NVA who were setting it up had fled as Graham approached. NVA were definitely in the area.

As night fell, though, guys moved around a bit to visit adjacent three-man positions, and quietly talked with Mike Gross's squad members. They told us that Ferrell had been walking point when he found a trail. Fearing an ambush, Mike had Ferrell take a direction slightly uphill from the trail. This, it turned out, saved the squad from a disaster. Shortly thereafter, the NVA opened up with claymores and AK's. The claymores had indeed been set up to rake the trail, and tore a path through the vegetation a whisker away from where the squad was positioned off to the side. The NVA appeared to have been taken by surprise almost as much as we were. Tom Cuffee, a big, muscular black guy from Virginia Beach who always behaved as if being big meant he should carry a heavier load, recounted how "the gooks were running from one bunker to the next, firing and then moving again, while a tripod-mounted "bigass" machine gun churned away." The squad kept their heads down as much as possible and crawled up on a line with the bunkers and slowly, carefully, began returning fire. They had wondered when the other '60's would be coming.

They got enough fire out, though, so that the NVA pulled back and headed into the jungle. As we would learn, this was the standard modus operandi for the NVA: even when in their own bunker complex, they would try to inflict some damage and then melt into the jungle before we could call in the deadly firepower of artillery and gunships.

51

No one knew who, if anyone, had been responsible for the KIA's and blood trail. They had all been firing as NVA flickered by between bunkers, and no one saw anyone hit.

Doc stopped by the three-man position I shared with Dixon and Rabenda. He was still wound up from the day's action. And he filled us in on why he was not there when we had returned to Pace's little command perimeter: Pace had ordered him to crawl up to Ferrell, but would not send even one rifleman from his perimeter to accompany him. So Doc had crawled by himself into the teeth of the automatic weapons fire, then patched up Ferrell's sucking chest wound.

"A medic is supposed to have infantry with him when he goes forward, "Doc told us. "We're not supposed to go by ourselves. It's SOP! Pace had to know this!"

As the night deepened, we remained on edge. We set up in our usual three-man positions, the positions forming a perimeter. But all that happened was a single rifle shot around midnight. My nerves must have been strung tighter than I wanted to believe, because after that lone shot, and for the only time in my army career, I fell asleep during my guard watch. I knew this because the next morning, Dixon, Rabenda, and myself all woke with the dawn, with no one on guard and waking the other two. Who had fallen asleep? It had to have been me, because the watch we passed around to time our hour of guard duty was in my hammock.

The next day, we once again set out through the jungle. During breaks, we smoked and talked. Anger at how Pace had neither sent any help to Gross's squad nor provided an escort for Doc bubbled up among us.

After two days, we were sent back to check out the base camp into which Ferrell had stumbled. The two dead NVA were still there, the 199th arm patches still stuck in their mouths where Lewis had put them when we left. We all thought that maybe this would perhaps frighten their comrades, if they had come back for the bodies. I can remember that the bodies were bloated and black. And I remember that they smelled frightful. But I must have blocked the memory of the smell from my mind, because to this day all I can remember is that it was awful, not how it actually smelled.

Disintegration
The rainy season was upon us, but our routine remained the same: head out into the jungle, do cloverleafs, and search a corridor of wilderness for the presence of NVA. We did occasionally work around the edges of rubber plantations and even a few isolated villages. The rain, which came twice every day, made it hard to keep trench foot and skin fungus at bay. Doc daily gave each of us a large white pill to help control our ringworm. One night, during a particularly hard rain, I simply screamed from pent-up frustration.

And we were bored -- for weeks sometimes, fighting through the jungle day after day, always slightly scared, but mostly knowing the next day, and the day after that, would be more of the same.

Our next contact with the enemy came when I was walking point. I came out of some scrubby jungle onto a downward-sloping field as long as a football field is wide, ending up against triple-canopy jungle. About halfway across, I notice a flash of movement in the tree line. I immediately flattened, and motioned behind me for everyone else to do the same. Then I saw movement again, and could see it was an NVA soldier.

I low-crawled back to Gallion and his RTO and whispered what I had seen. Gallion grabbed his handset and informed Pace, who was still back in the banana trees. Gallion listened a moment as Pace replied, then told me, "Pace wants you to get a better look, make sure of what you are seeing."

My imagination was kicking into high gear. If it were a base camp, I was exposed out here, and there would be claymores, maybe a machine gun. But I crawled forward a little farther. I could then pick out bunkers through the edge of the foliage. I crawled back to Gallion, told him, and heard him report it to Pace.

Pace ordered us to pull back. He said he was calling in a gunship strike. So we crawled back.

As we entered the little banana grove, we saw Pace set up a ways back with both machine guns close to him.

"Why the fuck aren't they here at the tree line?" Gallion grumbled under his breath. "If we were spotted, we'd have needed them to keep the gooks' heads down! We wouldn't have stood a chance."

Yes, I thought. When you needed suppressing fire, it was the continuous fire of the big gun that was required, not M16's with eighteen- or twenty-round clips. (The clips officially held twenty rounds but often jammed when loaded that full.) But I was too grateful to be off the open hillside to generate any real anger. Gallion and I lay prone, looking out from our tree line at the jungle where the base camp was.

After about ten tense minutes, we heard the *whop-whop* of a helicopter rotor, and a gunship -- a helicopter with big drums suspended beneath the airframe -- came in from my right, flying low. The big drums were mini-guns, electrically-powered machine guns that put out a hard-to-fathom number of rounds per second. After a moment of hovering about a hundred yards from where I had seen the bunkers, it gathered speed and flew directly over the spot. As it did, a sound almost like a long and extremely loud burp came from the vehicle, and the jungle underneath began churning with leaves and chopped-up branches. The chopper wheeled, made another firing run, and then flew away.

As the gunship departed, our squad got the order to move out and assault. The rest of the squad moved alongside Gallion and me, I pointed out where I had seen the bunkers, and we all emptied two or three clips into that area. Then silence: we were not receiving any return fire. If anyone had remained in the camp, we hoped either the gunship or our fusillade had killed them.

We quickly closed on the tree line, pushed through it, and dropped to the ground. Still silence. Gingerly, we crept forward, passing a couple of empty bunkers, a fire with a pot of rice cooking on it, and then some more bunkers. The ground, the bunkers, the little bit of vegetation between the bunkers, all were pockmarked with closely-spaced bullet holes. Why the cooking rice was untouched was a bit of a miracle, I thought. Gallion called Pace, told him it was clear, and the rest of the platoon came down the hill and joined us. Pace got on the radio and reported we had found a just-evacuated bunker complex. I could hear an agitated voice coming over the handset. Pace looked angry.

"They're mad we didn't get any bodies," he said to no one in particular. "We're to pursue aggressively." Looking around, he saw a trail leading away from the camp. "Gallion," he said, "take your squad and lead us down that trail."

Down a trail? We never take a trail! It's a recipe for walking into an ambush. No one was sent out on flank: Gallion tried to send them, but Pace stopped him, and said to move out now.

I was the point man, so off I went. I had always thought that when people talked about being so scared their knees were shaking, it was just an expression. But I now knew otherwise: my legs were literally shaking. Slowly, willing my legs to move, I followed the trail as it wound along a little stream bordered by a flat, grass-covered bank about ten feet wide on each side, with jungle beyond. My eyes scanned left and right, trying to make out any sign of a uniform, or any movement. I had no cover whatsoever.

After maybe fifteen minutes, maybe a half hour, but what seemed like a lifetime, Pace ordered a stop and gave us a compass heading to follow into the jungle. The craziness of following a path seemed to be over.

That night, talk again percolated from position to position in our NDP. I learned from the other squads that at my first report of an NVA, Pace had collected both of the squads' M60's around him, back in the cover of the banana trees. I complained bitterly about being made to follow a trail, knowing that the NVA had just minutes before moved down it. A common thought among those of us who had been with Lieutenant Walker was that he would not have let Battalion browbeat him into sending us along a trail into a likely ambush.

But we had not taken any casualties, and for the next few weeks we had no enemy contact. We grumbled about Pace, but the fear we had felt at what his leadership might mean for us diminished as we again became busy with the day-to-day challenges of living in the field: trying to keep from getting trench foot, worrying about our ringworm, struggling to keep our weapons and ammo clean, finding drinking water, and breaking trail through jungle underbrush and thicket-like savannahs, where the point man threw his body across the brush to break it down, a yard at a time, so we could move forward.

Then, one day we left the jungle and moved into an adjacent rubber plantation, where we set up for the night in our NDP. At dusk, a group of three or four NVA came walking toward our position. They were about a football field's distance away and had not noticed us. But we knew they would see us soon, because in the rubber plantation there was no vegetation on the ground to block their view. The trees themselves were aligned in long straight rows, affording clear views down the long columns between them. Lewis hurriedly got Jensen over to where there was a clear path between the trees to the approaching NVA, and had him fire a grenade. When firing the grenade launcher at a distant target, you point the barrel up at a high angle, and launch the grenade in a high parabolic arch. Jensen did this. And the grenade hit the branches high overhead, exploding harmlessly. But the NVA saw it explode, then saw us, and turned and ran back towards the jungle. We called in some artillery on the area where they were headed, but otherwise did not pursue them. We spent a tense night in our NDP: NVA were around.

The next morning, Battalion ordered us to head into the jungle where the NVA had fled the previous night. I was walking point. A few hundred yards into the jungle, I came across a small square latrine, much like what the point man for Gross's squad had found when we went to help Bravo a month or so earlier. Looking ahead down the trail that led from it, I saw an NVA some thirty feet away, not looking at me but crouched down, focused on doing something.

I sighted my rifle on him, then hesitated. Something in me did not want to shoot another human when he was not shooting at me. And after that brief hesitation, I also began thinking of other problems: were there claymores set up to defend the base camp that could be trained on me? I could not see clearly anywhere except down the trail. Were other bunkers close at hand, with machine guns ready to shoot me?

I turned around and clambered back to Mike Fields, who was filling in as squad leader while Gallion was in the rear taking the Sergeants Exam. I told Mike what I had seen. Then Jackson, who had been right behind me, said he had seen three NVA walking along to the side of us about thirty or forty feet away. We had come up against a base camp.

Fields got on the radio and reported to Pace. Pace told him we were pulling back to the rubber plantation, going back in opposite order, with us now the trailing squad.

Back in the rubber, Pace talked with Battalion. It appeared from what we could hear that they wanted to know if we were sure of what we had seen. A few minutes later, as we waited for orders, a Loach helicopter -- a small chopper that held the pilot and the Colonel who commanded our battalion in an observation-friendly Plexiglas bubble -- buzzed down over the NVA base camp area. After two or three low passes, we again pieced together from hearing Pace's side of the conversation that the Colonel did not see anything and would not authorize a gunship or artillery fire mission. We could tell from the loudness of the Colonel's voice that he was mad. We were ordered to go back and investigate on the ground.

I again walked point, back to where we had found the shitter. We then moved along the little path that ran from it until we reached a tree line, beyond which was an open area. Crouched in the edge of the vegetation, looking into the open area, I could see bunkers: it was a base camp.

I could not see any movement. Mike Fields came up next to me and offered to make the next move, into the camp. I told him no -- if I had opened fire when I first had a chance, it would all have been over by now. But I was scared. There was a clear gap between my hiding spot in the edge of the vegetation and the closest cover I could see: a termite mound, maybe three feet tall, with a base two or three feet wide. I gathered myself, and set off like a sprinter leaving the starting blocks towards the mound. But I was a sprinter with close to ninety pounds clanking around my pack frame and web gear. It was probably more like a shuffle.

As I dove headfirst towards the safety of the mound, an AK opened up, and rounds spattered the dirt around me. I flattened behind the mound. Then, as I started to raise my head to look over the top of the mound, a sapling growing out of the top of the mound was snipped off by the AK fire. My legs were splayed out behind me, and I felt something thumping my boots. I glanced back and saw dirt flying around my left boot. I quickly pulled it back to my right, into the cover of the mound. My steel pot, which was hanging from my waist on my web gear, jumped and danced as a bullet hit it. I slid my body even more to my right.

The fire was coming from off to my left, so I poked my M16 above the mound, holding it by its pistol grip, and returned fire without exposing my head. I just blindly sprayed, hoping to get the shooters to duck their heads and stop firing.

I could hear my squad along the edge of the vegetation behind me, moving in the direction of the firing and then starting to fire as well. People were yelling -- but what, I was not sure of. After our squad fired off a few clips, it seemed all of them were changing clips together, because there was a sudden silence. Why was I not hearing the continuous fire of the M60? Where was Cook?

After a moment, I realized the silence also meant the NVA were not firing. A few moments later, another squad moved up, spread out, and began moving along the other edge of the base camp, firing into each bunker and any bush behind which someone might hide. Eventually someone called "cease fire," and everyone looked to see if they saw any NVA.

Pace finally moved up to the edge of the vegetation and asked Fields what had happened. Fields told him that I had been first to return fire, and Pace asked me to point out where the enemy fire had come from. I did so, and Graham moved his squad up through the area to the bunkers I had been pointing at. A minute later he walked back and reported there were maybe a hundred shell casings on the bunker floor.

"Looks like they emptied a couple of clips and then didi-maoed," he said.

Again, we had been lucky: no casualties. The buzzing Loach undoubtedly had alerted the NVA that we were aware of the base camp, and they had moved out, leaving just a couple of men behind in a bunker. We were fortunate that their field of fire was hemmed in by another bunker, and they could not bring fire to bear on where my squad was stretched out in the tree line. If my squad had spread out in the other direction, the bullets that had missed me surely would have found others in my squad.

Pace was on the radio again. After putting the handset back on his RTO's web gear, he told Gallion we were heading out in pursuit, down a trail on the other side of the base camp where the two shooters had probably fled.

This time, every few yards the trail provided good opportunities for cover. So I set out, jumping from one little clump of brush to another. After a few hundred yards of this, Pace once again called an end to it, and we headed out along a compass heading into the jungle.

That night, Cook told me he had been kept back with Pace when my squad began its return to the base camp. At this no longer surprising news, I felt more fear than anger: I walked point, and chances were good that sooner or later the heavy continuous fire of the M60 would be needed to drive NVA away from my exposed position.

Time moved on. Weeks passed with no contact. Stinger re-upped: he felt like three more years in a safe job somewhere in the rear was a better bet than another six months of this. Tiny Glinka re-upped as well. His family had sent him the sad news that his new wife had filed for divorce and was living with another man.

One night we set up as a platoon on a night ambush, with Pace positioning us so that we had no choice but to sleep on the ground in a few inches of water. As we awoke at dawn of the next day and began heating our C rations and coffee with burning C4, low-volume conversations moved from position to position: was anyone mad enough to kill Pace?

The prevailing sentiment was that it would be a good idea, and justified, to kill him. But almost all of us said we wouldn't do it ourselves. Still, the question floated in the air: if someone else did, would anyone turn him in?

The two candidates for actually doing the deed were Harvey Sixkiller and Richnell. They were the two survivors of the ambush that had immediately preceded my arrival into the platoon, and they were very close friends. And they seemed now just a little bit crazy enough to actually kill Pace. Both seemed contemplative when asked whether they could do it.

But one platoon member, Martin Clay, made it clear: if he saw someone kill Pace, he would turn him in. He agreed Pace was a danger to us, but he wouldn't let someone kill him.

The idea faded away. But it illustrated how much we disliked the man, how cowardly we believed him to be. The about-face from volunteering to walk point into a base camp to pulling the '60's back with him when we had a firefight was not only repellent, but dangerous.

And danger we would see again. On August 20, as the rainy season began to taper off, our whole company was air-lifted to an operation in an area thick with jungle and with NVA. At every turn, it seemed a squad was encountering an NVA squad. Coming out of jungle into a clearing, we literally bumped into an NVA squad, and Richnell was shot in the side in the ensuing exchange of fire. Hours later, we emerged into an old logging road, looked down it, and saw another squad of NVA, carrying bags of rice on their shoulders. Thankfully, at least from our perspective, they dropped the rice and ran. Then, two members of first platoon were killed when we again ran into a platoon of NVA. One of them, Jackie Byrd, was a slender kid who was proud of the fact that he did not have to shave. "I'm smooooth," he'd say. "Ain't got to waste my time shaving." In the firefight, he rolled up on his side from his prone position to get a new clip for his M16, and a round went right through his temple.

After two days, we had suffered six casualties: two KIA and four seriously wounded, one of whom would die back in the hospital. Bill Preston, who had ten days left in the field before his year was done, insisted on being allowed to ride back to Brigade Main Base on the outbound resupply chopper so he could re-enlist and get out of the field. And two guys from first platoon had an "accident": one of them discharged his rifle, conveniently taking off one finger from both his and his buddy's hand. Martin Clay was sent to the rear because he was walking around with a round chambered in his M16 and the safety off, preparing to fire at imaginary sounds: a danger to us all.

We were a nervous and scared group.

That night, as we set up for our NDP, Pace sliced his shin with his machete. He made Doc check it out. Doc said a band aid was all that was required. Pace insisted it was worse than that, and he told the Captain he felt he needed to go back to headquarters on the outgoing resupply chopper that was about to land. The Captain, we were told, appeared skeptical, but demurred.

We never saw Pace again.

Of course, it wasn't because his cut turned out to be worse than it had appeared. What we heard from the company clerk was that every time he was scheduled to rejoin us, he would come up with another ailment, apparently hard to diagnose, and have to remain in the rear.

Chapter Five

Thanksgiving

With Sergeant Lewis now leading the platoon, we continued patrolling. But as we moved into October, we noticed some changes. First, we worked around villages a little more. We were told that these were "known VC" villages, because they had no fighting-age men in them, and none of these missing men were in the ARVN, the South Vietnamese army. We patrolled through the jungles and the rubber and coffee plantations that surrounded these villages, hoping to intercept the VC leaving and returning to their homes.

Second, we sometimes worked with ARVN forces, which were stationed in small mud-and-sandbag forts right outside the villages we worked around. The ARVN soldiers were natural antagonists of the VC-sympathizing villagers. Left to their own devices, they seemed happy to stay within a short distance of their forts. But we were now implementing the "Vietnamization" of the war, and went on joint operations with the ARVN in order to help them get ready to take over the fighting. We did not think much of the ARVN: most of our observation had been that they were disinclined to undertake the dangerous task of searching the surrounding area for VC and NVA. In retrospect, we probably didn't appreciate their lot: drafted for the duration of a war with no end in sight, and poorly equipped and poorly led.

But this sort of duty seemed less dangerous than traipsing through deep jungle in the hope (of our superiors, at least) that we would stumble upon NVA elements. And in fact, our combat experience in this duty was exceptionally one-sided.

On a joint patrol with the local ARVN, we were circling a village along a road that ran next to a coffee plantation on our left and a small strip of trees and brush on the village side. A shoulder-high bank edged the road on the village side. With unfortunate and fatal timing, a young VC carrying a rifle jumped out of the brush on the village side, heading across the road, undoubtedly en route to rejoin his VC cadre. He regained his balance from his jump, then glanced to his left. His eyes widened in fear and his jaw dropped as he saw us. All of us at the head of the column, ARVN and GI alike, raised our weapons and opened fire on full automatic. Our young VC made one step towards the coffee plantation before stumbling forward, his body twitching as multiple rounds hit him.

We found him a yard or so into the coffee, dead. He lay prone on his stomach, his head turned slightly to the left, his open mouth full of the loose soil of the plantation. Bullets had torn through his torso and his legs.

The ARVN were jabbering in their own language, obviously excited. Gallion came up to me and we looked at the dead VC. He was so young-looking, and his rifle looked ancient, like something from WWI. Maybe it was the gleeful attitude of the ARVN, but for the first time since we had been in Vietnam, Gallion grimaced at the sight.

"You know, "he said, "he's like us, really. Has a mom, maybe a girlfriend."

I silently agreed. The weight of the dead was starting to accumulate on us. The ARVN cut down a small sapling, then hung the dead VC on it, tying his wrists together over one end and his feet over the other. Like a dead deer. Two of the ARVN hoisted the pole between them, over their shoulders, and their entire contingent started down the road towards the village.

"They know him, and his family," our interpreter told us. We formed up and followed them into the village. They stopped in front of a house, really a three-sided one-room building with a thatched roof and pigs penned in a crawlspace beneath it. The two ARVN holding the pole took it off of their shoulders, then swung it a few times to build momentum, and then threw it right in front of the house. They were all yelling and gesticulating-shaking fists and pointing at the house.

The ARVN then turned around and went back to their fort at the edge of the village. We went down the road as well, but continued out of the village, heading to an NDP somewhere away from the ARVN.

Deeper into October a new Second Lieutenant was assigned to us. We were his first combat command, and he vacillated between trying to be friendly and trying to be a hardass leader. For whatever reason, he was recalled after a few weeks, and Lewis again became Platoon Leader.

Around this time our company got a two-day "Stand Down." We were sent back to Brigade Main Base, given new fresh uniforms, cots in a barracks to sleep in, and two days with no responsibility except to show up for Reveille in the morning. The company Sergeant Major organized a strip show for us one night, and we went to the EM club the other night, where we learned that racial tensions were high back in the rear.

Dixon, Rabenda, Jackson, Cook, and I all went. We were as much of a family as one might imagine: We lived together twenty-four hours a day, seven days a week, and depended on each other, at times, for our very lives. Shortly after we sat down together at a table, we noticed we were the only integrated table. After a moment, a black guy came over and talked to Cook and Jackson.

"Why don't ya'll come over with the brothers?"

With little embarrassed smiles, Jackson and Cook said no. The fellow then became more insistent, calling on them to show solidarity. When they still declined, he gave them an exasperated look, then a sneer, and left.

I have never forgotten how our small group, all from very different backgrounds, and all returning (if we were lucky) to very different futures, became bound to each other by our shared hardships and dangers. For those few months of our lives, color really didn't matter.

I found the Brigade library, a small hut, and read *Catch-22* over those two days, identifying with Yossarian. I also read an old issue of our Brigade's newspaper, which until then I had not known existed. It featured upbeat articles about how some company's point man had killed a Boa Constrictor, and about how another had happened across an NVA and quickly shot him. Most interesting to me was an article reporting our firefight when Farrell had been shot: the two KIA and one blood trail that we had reported had expanded to ten KIA's, according to a quote from some officer at Battalion.

I went to Bangkok for a week of R and R. As the return flight took off, heading back to Tan Son Nhut air base, I experienced a wave of deep longing for a normal life, in which I would go to school or a job and would come home every night to friends or family with whom I would play cards or watch television or just talk, about anything other than NVA and bad officers and jungle rot.

Rejoining the platoon at the end of October, I realized I was the most senior member of the platoon, except for Gallion, now a sergeant and unlikely to get out of the field, and Morehead Sam. Doc Clary had got a job in the rear. I began to let myself hope that before long a job in the rear would open up and it would be mine.

November was turning out to be uneventful: we tromped around the countryside, set up ambushes that never were sprung, and listened (with hope that they were true) to rumors that the whole 199th was going to be shipped home in January.

But on Thanksgiving, our platoon walked out of the jungle onto a road that bordered a coffee plantation. We were going to be re-supplied at a wide spot in the road where a chopper could hover; later, trucks were to bring us a hot Thanksgiving meal.

We set up a perimeter about fifty yards from the re-supply spot, spanning the road. If you can picture a clock superimposed over the road, with the road running from 9:00 o'clock straight across to 3:00, my squad was set up as follows: Rabenda was at 10:30, Dixon at 9:30, and I was just off the road at 8:30. Ring, an FNG, was at 8:00, another FNG at 7:30, and Cook with the M60 was at 7:00.

The resupply spot was straight down the road about feet from 9:00. Gallion, Jackson, and Dewitt were all in the rear; Gallion and Jackson were on R and R and Dewitt had malaria.

We heard the *whop-whop-whop* of the chopper and two guys from another squad went out and helped pull the supplies off, which were mostly C rations. After the chopper left, they watched over the pile of boxes while we all took turns going and getting our share. In my squad, we went counterclockwise, with Rabenda starting, then Dixon, then me.

When my turn came, I went down the road, grabbed six C rations, and headed back. As I turned off the road, I saw that Jesse and Richard were busily arranging their new C rations in their packs. I had situated myself under a tree, between some big exposed roots, and I sat down and began to do the same.

Suddenly splitting the still air came an enormous explosion, with something -- shrapnel, I quickly guessed -- chopping leaves and twigs from the tree branch over my head. Then came the *tat-tat-tat* sound of AK's, with dirt flying up all around me. I flattened out, anxiously looking across the road beyond Dixon, where it seemed the fire was coming from. Dixon was groaning, leaned up against a tree. Then Cook came by running full-tilt, heading with his M60 toward the sound of the AK's. As he flattened out in the ditch that bordered the road, I grabbed my belt of 60 ammo and moved up next to him. He began walking his fire in arcs from side to side, and I fed a new belt into the gun after the first hundred rounds were gone. We couldn't see any targets through the coffee trees but hoped the fire was driving them off.

It must have. We heard the AK's stop, then we ceased fire. Silence. I looked over at Dixon, ten feet from me. He was moaning, and a bright red arc of blood pulsated from his leg, making a five-foot high parabola like the St. Louis Arch, then dying off, then recreating itself every second. Our new medic, a six-foot-three refrigerator who had volunteered to leave a safe job in the rear so as to see what it was like in the field, ran up and slid down next to Dixon, then called me over:

"Can you help?"

Still worried that NVA were around, I low-crawled over. By the time I got there, the medic was pressing down on the top of Dixon's thigh with both hands, and the arterial arch had stopped.

"When I move my hands, "he told me, "put yours in the same spot and push down hard."

He moved his hands, and I stuck mine down in their place. Dickie's thigh was gashed open, and I was putting my hands into a glistening, jelly-like, pink-and-white variegated slab of flesh, with the arterial blood just starting to well up before I got my hands down.

I pushed hard, and our medic began doing something to Dickie's upper abdomen, which was also hit. After somehow stopping the bleeding there, he moved down to Dickie's calf muscle, which looked as if it had been put through a cheese grater.

After doing something down there for a minute, he said, "OK, let up."

I did, and the artery did not bleed. I remember being surprised that pressure alone could stop such a powerful arterial flow.

I moved back from Dixon. The medic did something more to the artery and then jogged towards Rabenda. Dickie was still moaning, obviously in terrible pain. But now I realized Rabenda was also moaning loudly, lying on his side, and clutching his belly.

He had been hit in the stomach. The medic put some bandages on him, then jogged across the perimeter to where my squad's FNG, whose name I can never remember, was lying clutching his leg. He had a bullet wound in his thigh.

I moved back to where Cook was still peering into the coffee trees and saw our other FNG, Dennis Ring, over in his position, holding his wrist. I moved over, no longer crawling, and he raised his left wrist. A neat small furrow the diameter of a pencil ran through the side of it.

"Looks like a claymore pellet," I said. "See Doc when he gets a moment." Sergeant Lewis was now in the middle of the perimeter, on the radio, arranging a dust-off. I helped put Dixon on a poncho liner and pulled him into the interior of the perimeter, while others did the same for Rabenda and the FNG with the leg wound. Dixon was making awful groans, as was Rabenda.

The leg-wounded guy was pretty quiet, and not in as much pain.

It turned out that Lewis had sent a squad to patrol the perimeter so we could claim a secure Landing Zone –"LZ" -- for the dust off. I must have missed the order, because I looked down between a row of coffee trees, saw what I thought were NVA, and raised my weapon.

"Hey, that's Mike Bass's squad!" someone who saw me cried out. "They're patrolling the perimeter."

I lowered my rifle, and we discussed the miscommunication. But Mike and his squad were in no danger: while trying to sight, I had got the shakes. The sight on the front of my rifle barrel jumped so much I would have missed by ten feet.

Cook and I then took Lewis out towards where we thought the attack had come from, just beyond Dixon and Rabenda's position. Thirty feet or so beyond their position, we found a twenty-foot long tongue of burned grass with the wider base farthest away from our position. We figured then that the NVA had crept up and set off a big Chicom Claymore. They had then strafed our position with AK's, probably until Cook started returning fire.

The medivac chopper seemed to take a long time. Dixon eventually lost consciousness. To my shame, I realized I was relieved: his moans and obvious pain were unnerving me.

We eventually got everybody on the chopper. Then we got the order to saddle up: we were moving a little farther down the road. As we moved, we passed a small structure along the side of the road that resembled a giant hutch like the one in which my grandmother displayed her china. Arranged on its shelves were religious-looking objects of porcelain.

As Lewis passed, he suddenly turned, took his rifle butt, and swept it across shelf after shelf, smashing the porcelain until it was all broken. He then took a deep breath, and continued down the road, still scowling.

Like Lewis, we were all unsettled, frustrated, and angry. Had our perimeter been too lax? It would be hard to say: coffee trees were maybe ten to fifteen feet tall, clear of branches for the first five feet or so, but bushy above that. That meant you could see between two rows of trees but not much in the adjacent rows.

The anger and frustration were about the whole enterprise, however. Why were we here, when the locals in the areas in which we had been clearly supported the North? Why did the ARVN need to be pushed to go out of their forts and do the dangerous job of trying to kill the NVA?

In October, we had been trucked into a big flat basin, covered with soy beans, surrounded by jungle. Again, we were told that it was a Viet Cong village and that we were to interdict the VC as they moved back and forth from the jungle to the village. And indeed, first platoon had seen and killed a lone VC making the trek across the open fields.

But more interesting, a chopper had brought a television crew out. An interviewer -- some guys said it was Morley Safer, maybe it was Sam Donaldson -- told us there were giant peace protests being held that month in the U.S. What did we think about it?

Everyone I heard respond said something like what Mike Bass said. A Mississippian who likely had never heard any of the arguments against the war, he answered, "Hell, if they're for ending this shit, I'm for 'em."

The basic argument put forth by the Army as they tried to motivate us to fight had been something along the lines of "We're helping the South Vietnamese kick out the communist invaders." I think we were all angry about losing our friends in a war whose motivation seemed far removed from that official explanation.

A little later on that Thanksgiving, we stopped, set up a perimeter, and watched trucks come down the road and stop in our center. The company's Sergeant-Major hopped down, and cooks unloaded insulated canisters of food and set up a buffet line of sorts. We took turns coming off our position for turkey, mashed potatoes, gravy, and cranberry sauce, along with a "good job" and handshake from "Top," the company Sergeant Major. I should have been used to it by then, but the juxtaposition of the recent firefight with the associated blood and painful moans of the wounded, and the Thanksgiving dinner -- which seemed to emphasize that firefights were all in a day's work -- seemed surreal, like a dream.

That night, as we set up in our NDP, some of the platoon members talked to me about how I had not been hit, while the positions on all sides of me were. Was it, they asked, my field savvy in making sure I was partially protected by a tree? I had been in Vietnam a long time, and was viewed as the seasoned veteran, I guess. I told them the truth: dumb luck. What I really wished for, I told them, was Ring's injury: all I needed was one more purple heart, for no matter how small a scratch, and I was back in the rear. I did not need what we called the "million dollar wound," a wound that got you back to the World and ended your own personal war.

A million dollar wound

The next morning, we saddled up and headed into the coffee plantation. We were moving quietly, knowing NVA were in the area. About 8:30, Lewis positioned us thirty feet from a slightly raised road in an L-shaped ambush. He had my squad, which now consisted of Cook and me, as the short leg of the "L," along a gentle bend in the road. The rest of the platoon stretched out to our right at a shallow angle. We could see the squad setting up claymores that would rake the road.

I propped myself up alongside a coffee tree on my right, facing the road, using my pack as a chair back, with my legs bent in front of me. Cook was maybe eight feet to my left. It was, as usual, a hot, perfectly still morning. No cover was available: the ground was as flat as a table top, and the trunks of the coffee trees were no more than two inches thick. Big ants crawled around my feet, threatening to climb up my legs.

For about twenty minutes, we waited. I tracked the progress of the ants as they explored up my boots. Then, noiselessly, a soldier -- not VC but NVA, with a true uniform down to his bloused pants tucked into his laced-up boots -- heading from right to left down the road, entered my vision as his frame cleared the visual obstruction of the coffee tree on my right. My heart thumped. I turned my head imperceptibly, I hoped, and checked in my peripheral vision that Cook was also focused on the road. The NVA soldier was walking slowly and deliberately, scanning left and right. He hadn't seen us yet.

About ten feet behind him, a second soldier came into view. By now, I was ever-so-slowly moving my selector switch off safety to full automatic. The little *snick* sound it made seemed so, so loud to me that I was afraid the NVA could hear it.

But with two in our vision, Cook opened the ambush. His M60 gave its characteristic barking, staccato sound, and the first NVA was literally picked up by the bullets and driven horizontally off the road, landing motionless on the other side. The second NVA, with incredible quickness, flattened out on our side of the road, aiming an RPG at Cook and me. We were so close I could see his eyes looking down the RPG tube. They looked fierce, flat and black, unafraid. I remember thinking: This is not his first firefight.

I had fired off one or two rounds -- my rifle seemed to jam, or maybe I had only got the selector switch to semi-automatic -- when a round went through my left side, front to back, spinning me in a counterclockwise direction. My upper body went numb. But I was still looking directly at the soldier with the RPG, and was now yelling "Get him, Cook!" as I couldn't seem to pull my trigger anymore. Then the numbness left and a wave of pain washed through me.

Immediately, an explosion went off between me and Cook, and I went flying into leaves of the coffee tree. I saw leaves, and sky, and then landed on the ground. Everything seemed tilted at a ninety degree angle.

A moment later, my visionary plane returned to normal, I heard claymores exploding and M16's on full automatic. Good, I thought, the NVA are on the run, and the medic can help me. And here he came, running full tilt through the coffee trees.

I knew I was hurt but thought I was doing OK: I had seen people shot, and my belief was if you were conscious, you were going to be all right. Then my bowels spasmed, and the medic was doing something to my chest. A sliver of doubt intruded into my mind: maybe I was hurt worse than I had originally thought.

"Two KIA's," I heard someone say, and someone was talking about getting a dust off.

Soon I was lying flat on the deck of a chopper. I was surely in shock, but I was still conscious enough to realize that Cook was sitting next to me, legs dangling outside the chopper.

We landed, people put me on a wheeled stretcher, took me, I think, for a quick x-ray, and then I was in a brightly lit room, with a masked doctor looking intently down at me. Suddenly he frowned.

"His chest is filling up with blood!"

I felt an intense burning in my chest and lost consciousness.

When I next woke up, the same doctor was again looking down at me.

"Well, we weren't sure you were going to make it," he said.

I slowly began to notice my surroundings. I lay in a bed with my torso slightly raised, in a brightly-lit ward, its walls wooden like a barracks. What I learned was a respirator had been hooked up to me through a tracheotomy in my neck, and a large glass jar was connected to my chest via a plastic tube. A nurse and another medic also hovered over me.

"Do you remember the operating room?" the doctor asked. "You don't have speak, you probably can't with the respirator. Just nod."

I nodded. I also tried to say yes -- and successfully, I thought, croaked out a whispered version of it.

"Well, the artery in your chest that carries blood to your arm was nicked by the bullet, and gave way just as we got you on the operating table. I opened your chest without anesthesia. Did you feel it? A burning, maybe?"

Yes, a little, I croaked. He went on about how sorry he was to have had to do that; he seemed really worried that that was the worst part of the whole experience. I wanted to assure him it wasn't, but I couldn't muster the energy to talk.

He went on to explain my condition. The artery to my arm was gone, but my arm should still have enough collateral circulation so that amputation would be unnecessary. I had lost a lobe of my lung, but that wasn't a big concern. And the doctor's worry that I might not make it had come from my loss of blood before they got the artery "tied off."

"You had a couple of cardiac arrests -- from loss of blood, no damage to your heart. We were afraid we'd run out of blood for transfusions. You took thirty units of blood!

"If we had gotten you even a minute or two later," the doctor continued, "we probably would have lost you. Bullet fragments had perforated your subclavian artery, close to the aorta. The artery gave way just as we had you on the table. You're a fortunate soldier."

Indeed I was, I thought. The platoon had been quick to secure an LZ, and the dust off had come quick. If it had taken as long as it had the previous day, I would not have made it.

But I was alive. I wiggled the big toe on my left foot. It felt exhilarating to be able to do it. I was tired, hooked up to machines -- but looking forward, it seemed, to a full recovery, with all appendages intact.

And over the next week I improved. I found that a day had passed between surgery and my waking up. After a few more days, my temperature spiked and they wrapped me in refrigerated blankets, but apart from that, I felt better every day. The second day, a nurse wrote a letter to my parents -- I couldn't hold a pen yet -- telling them I'd been hit, but not too serious, and I was in the 24th Evac hospital:

Dear Folks,

Hi there! I thought I'd fill you in on the latest wrinkle over here. Seems like I caught a bullet in my shoulder and will be home sooner than I expected. Don't worry, it's just a scratch, but it will probably get me home. No sweat. I'm writing this in hopes we won't have the same problems we had last time.

I'm at the 24th Evac Hospital right now. Will probably be here a week or so, then probably Japan, then home. Don't bet on it, but that's the way it looks now. Look for me when you see me. Probably be best not to write till you hear from me again.

Love,

Bob

I didn't know until later that the Army had sent a series of telegrams to my family starting shortly after my surgery, telling them I was "critically wounded" with "cause for concern." Now, having my own children, I can understand the fear my parents felt during those early days after my wound. With no email and no long-distance phone availability, all they had was a daily telegram that for a week kept telling them there was "cause for concern."

After two days, I was off the ventilator, breathing on my own, and I could move around in a wheelchair and visit my buddies. In the next ward were Dixon, Rabenda, and the FNG with the leg wound. Dickie wasn't able to sit up, and his heavily-wrapped legs were suspended from some traction device. He got a morphine shot every four hours. His face looked pained, and all he could talk about was how long would it be before he could get more morphine. Jesse was better off, but still in a lot of pain; abdominal wounds, I was told, were notoriously painful. The FNG was in pretty good shape: his femur had a slight fracture, but he was expected to go to the convalescence center at Cam Rhan Bay. Cook's wounds must have been slight. He had already been sent there.

Lewis came by. He looked uncomfortable. The last few days had shaken him, I thought. I had always thought, and still did, that he was a decisive but careful leader. But I think the responsibility of being in charge weighed on him.

Doc Clary visited as well. He said the rumor from the company was that I'd lost my arm. I was happy to show him the rumor was not true. He left me a paperback copy of *The Sot-Weed Factor*, a novel by John Barth. I ended up reading everything Barth wrote.

After about a week, the tube that had emptied into the big glass jar I carried around was removed from my chest and I was shipped off to Japan. My first night there was in a ward occupied only by me and a totally gauze-swathed guy suspended in a "Stryker" frame: a big wheel with a stretcher across its diameter on which the guy was strapped. Someone came in every few hours and rotated the angle of his stretcher. A nurse told me he was a burn patient, and was not able to speak yet. I felt better about what had happened to me. It could have been worse.

They moved me the next day to a ward where everyone was ambulatory. My throat still had a hole in it through which I coughed bloody clots of phlegm that hit the sheets of the guy across the aisle from me. But we all had our problems, and he, I, and the nurse laughed about it.

One night I had a vivid dream. In it, I was re-living a real experience I had while rabbit hunting with my grandfather. We were moving through clumps of brush on a pasture on my great-grandfather's farm. I was twelve: the age at which my relatives thought I was trustworthy enough to hunt rabbits with them. I kicked at a brush pile and a rabbit came out the other side, zigging and zagging away. I shouldered my shotgun, pointed, and fired.

One pellet caught the rabbit in a leg, breaking it. I ran up on it. It was dragging its broken leg along as it tried to pull forward. I felt queasy: I had never been this close to a wounded animal, and I wanted to undo what I had done to this creature. Knowing I couldn't do that, I raised my shotgun and prepared to put the rabbit out of its pain. My grandfather told me not to: it would get more shot in the meat. I always wanted the approval of my grandfather, and I dutifully (if squeamishly) stepped on its neck. As the rabbit died, its bladder emptied on the ground at my feet.

In the hospital in Japan, when the rabbit died in my dream, I suddenly felt as if I too were dying, with something slipping away inside me, and my bladder emptied as well. I awoke peeing in the bed, my heart pounding.

I called a nurse for help, and she came over, got new bedding, and helped me re-make the bed without a hint of embarrassment.

For years, I never had another dream about Vietnam. I believed that whatever fears of death I'd had were purged that night.

On the evening of December 22, I was loaded, on a stretcher, with a hundred or so other wounded GI's in a big cargo plane and sent to Andrews Air Force Base outside of Washington DC. There we were loaded on a bus and carried to Walter Reed Medical Center in DC. I was home for Christmas.

Chapter Six

Walter Reed

A doctor came by my room at Walter Reed. He checked my various scars, which were for the most part healed over. He told me I would be allowed to go home for Christmas, and when I returned the Army would begin processing my medical discharge.

My Dad picked me up on the 24th, and we drove the forty miles to Baltimore. Dad seemed different to me. I didn't sense what I had always felt to be his disapproval: disapproval of my risky and impetuous choices, of my lack of planning and foresight, and of my desire to be part of a bigger world than the one circumscribed by our Southern family. He seemed simply glad to have me back. Dad was not—and never became -- a "warm and fuzzy" type: never in my life would he say "I love you "or hug me. But riding home from Walter Reed, I began to realize how scared he had been and how much he would have missed me.

I still had some dressings to change, and my voice was weak and rough-sounding, but I was home. It was a great gift for my family and for me. I talked by phone with my sister and with my grandparents.

Before I returned to Walter Reed, I attended the wedding of my best friend from high school. We joked about how it meant so much to me to get back for his wedding that I went and got shot.

But what I remember most was how it seemed to me that most of my old friends were uneasy around me. My voice was hoarse, as I learned it would be for the rest of my life, and my tracheotomy scar was still raw. I also weighed thirty pounds less than I had in high school.

I couldn't quite get over how life for all these people was so, well, normal. Didn't they know people were dying daily? Weren't they a little ashamed at being so wrapped up in trivial stuff like so-and-so's new car?

And of course my ex-girlfriend's best friend, Rhonda, was there. We had always been friends, and she told me about my ex's new boyfriend. She leveled with me: my old girlfriend knew I was back but didn't want to see me. I began to see how my fantasy of being irresistible to women because of my veteran status was just that -- a fantasy.

A few days later I was back at Walter Reed, where my doctor told me a vascular surgeon wanted to see me. Colonel Rich, the surgeon, explained that he thought he could take a vein from my leg and use it as a replacement for the artery that had been shot away. I would once again have arterial flow to my arm. My arm wouldn't feel as cold, and it would be stronger.

So they stopped work on my medical discharge and put me in the surgical ward. Over the next two months, they would map my existing blood flow by shooting radioactive dye through my arteries, and plan the repair surgery.

I now had a new Army home, the surgical ward at Walter Reed. It was a plain room lined with about twenty beds along each wall. With one exception, everyone was awaiting surgery (or a series of surgeries) or recuperating.

The exception was a cheerful fellow who helped out with some of the chores around the ward but had no scheduled surgeries and was not officially recuperating. He did, though, have a mass of scars over his somewhat-distended belly.

After introducing himself, he explained his situation. After his surgeries, he had been placed in "the annex": a separate building for almost-recuperated patients, where everyone had nightly passes and could go out and partake of DC's nightlife. While generally a peaceable and cheerful person, he occasionally became enraged at civilians for reasons he could not remember afterwards. One night outside of a nightclub he had kicked some civilian's head into a curb, again and again. The doctors decided he needed to stay where he could be supervised while they worked on his emotional state, so they kept him on the surgical ward. As was universal among us, our conversational icebreakers were about what had happened to us: the details of a firefight, or a mortar attack, or an ambush, or a helicopter crash. So it was between me and our orderly. He explained to me that he had been a "LRRP," a member of a four-man long-range reconnaissance patrol. These elite units were dropped deep in the jungle, where they located enemy units and reported their locations. Needless to say, this was dangerous duty. Our orderly's stomach wounds had come from a machine gun.

"We were being extracted by chopper," he explained. "The gook's must have heard the chopper, and were waiting for us. I got four rounds in the stomach before they pulled me on the chopper." It was his fourth purple heart, he said. His mind had "just not been right since," he told me.

My days were spent in the Day Room, where the scores of us who were ambulatory went and watched television, read, or played bumper pool. Once again I realized how lucky I was: so many other patients had large depressions in their skulls, or had arms pulled up and attached to facial wounds to create skin grafts, or were missing arms or hands altogether, or hobbled around with a missing limb or other injury. One of the hobblers turned out to be someone from Baltimore with whom I had been drafted and with whom I had been in Basic training. We became good friends. He had been shot in the knee and would forever limp. But like all of us, he was looking forward to being out of the army and starting a civilian life.

All of us who had been wounded in combat (which was almost all of us) had a positive attitude as we looked forward to a civilian life once more. One guy from Brooklyn was missing his leg below the knee and would always have a colostomy bag. But he was excited about his plan to use his disability money to own a bar back home. A West Virginian -- almost a caricature of a hillbilly with his thin tall body and overbite face -- was fighting through multiple surgeries to try and save his leg. He wanted to farm again, and to hunt on the mountainsides of West Virginia, he said, and that could not happen if he lost his leg. The wheelchair corps of double-leg amputees ran races down the ramps that went from the upper to lower floors, laughing as they careened around corners.

We were motivated. We had survived, and we wanted to move on. Later, I would learn that another phase followed this first one, a phase in which anger and resentment moved in.

The one non-combat-wounded patient I knew was put in the bed beside me in late January. He told me he had an esophageal hernia that needed surgical repair. Then he somewhat sheepishly told me his duty had been on a Caribbean island, manning satellite-tracking radar of some sort.

He had his surgery and was returned to the bed beside me. He began complaining immediately, and then daily, about the pain. The surgeon explained it would take some time to get better, but the surgery had been successful and he would have a full recovery. But he moaned and complained almost non-stop, day after day. He was told to get up and walk, but he wouldn't, saying it hurt too bad. On rounds, the surgeon began to look exacerbated as my neighbor whined about the pain.

He'd had some surgery, yes, and it hurt, of course. But where was his fight? The rest of us knew the pain from wounds and surgeries but fought to get better, walking around with our IV stands as soon as possible, knowing it was important to our recovery.

And my neighbor got worse and worse, and eventually died. The orderlies told me that the doctors believed it was not because the surgery was bad, but because he gave up fighting. I felt little sympathy for him.

My surgery was done in March. It took nine hours but was successful: the doctors took a vein from my leg and connected my left brachial artery with my left carotid, giving me arterial blood flow to my arm.

I remained at Walter Reed until my discharge on May 22, 1970. That day, I walked out the front doors and looked over a bright sunny lawn that sloped down to the bus stop that would take me to downtown DC. There I would catch the Greyhound bus to Baltimore. I was a civilian, I and doubted I would ever again experience the sense of freedom and possibility that I felt that day. My life was in front of me, and I knew I would never again have to do anything as hard as the Army. I thought my war was finally over.

Chapter Seven

That Close

I went back to Michigan State that summer, eventually graduated, and then went on to get my Ph.D. in Economics from The Johns Hopkins University. I thought of myself as fundamentally unaffected by Vietnam. Yes, I jumped at fireworks, jerked myself awake as I fell asleep, afraid that I was falling asleep on guard duty, and experienced adrenaline rushes from the *whop-whop* of an approaching helicopter. But I only had dreams and memories on the rare occasions when I drank a lot.

While still at Michigan State, in the spring of 1971, I went to Washington DC to participate in Operation Dewey Canyon III, a peace protest by the Vietnam Veterans against the War. While there, camping on the National Mall (despite a Justice Department order not to do so), I ran into Doc Clary.

Doc, it turned out, was going to college in Georgetown. We caught up, ragged on Pace a little, drank some wine from a communal bottle passed between us and Ted Kennedy, who stayed the night with us, and went our separate ways.

Later, while at Hopkins, I reconnected with Doc by chance. I had noticed an advertisement on the Hopkins campus for a poetry reading at the Maryland Poetry Society by Patrick Clary. I went, the poet was indeed Doc, and we drank some beers, relived some Vietnam stories, and again went our separate ways. But we vowed to remain in touch.

And we did. So when I let Doc know I was teaching in Davis, California, he told me it was the town in which he had grown up. Doc and I arranged for him to visit. It was the spring of 1981. I picked Doc up at the Sacramento airport. At Doc's direction, I stopped to buy gin and tonic, then continued on home. Over the next few days, Doc visited old friends, told me about how his first wife's two sisters -- all daughters of the Davis Methodist minister -- had died at Jonestown "drinking the Kool-Aid" as wives of the cult leader Jim Jones, and introduced me to Gin and Tonics.

One evening, drinking gin and tonics on our back patio in the dry breeze that every night came up the Sacramento river and caused Central Valley temperatures to drop from over 100 to the 50's, our talk turned to Vietnam. We relived how Pace had made Doc crawl through fire without any help to aid Ferrell, and how Pace had pulled the M60's back to him every firefight after his first, the one in which by rights he should have been killed.

I mused about how I often wondered whether Pace had really had courage at the start -- or had never had it, and just lacked the imagination to know how risky our world was going to be. I opined he must have had courage once, because my booby trap had surely shown him how dangerous our lives were. And foolish as it was, he had volunteered for that mission.

"Oh no," Doc said. "You know, don't you, that I had to set up with him in our NDP's most nights. I was stuck with him. He talked about the booby trap more than a few times. He told me he thought it was just carelessness on your part that led to you being wounded."

"How so?"

"Well, he said all you needed to do was be better about picking up your feet, like he did. He said three people had stepped along that dike before you."

I fumed. I had been carrying the PRC-25, spare batteries, all my other gear, and even his rifle, his helmet -- and his cigarettes! Of course it was easier for him to pick up his feet.

"What a prick!" I told Doc. "You know, there's no justice. The sorry shit never even got hit over there!"

"Oh no," said Doc. "He was hit when you were. He said he never put in for a purple heart, but said he was nicked in the head by shrapnel."

"Bullshit! He was too far down the trail when I hit the mine. Fields had found another booby trap up the dike, and he had practically ran up to see it."

"No, he was pretty persuasive. We'd be set up at night, he'd tell me about how you tripped the booby trap, and then he would stick his finger through this shell hole in his steel pot and wiggle it at me. 'That close, Doc,' he'd say."

I exploded with laughter. "That asshole! Doc, I was carrying his helmet -- it was nowhere near him or his head!"

Doc looked stunned. After a few minutes, he said, "Well, that fits, doesn't it. He was such a dick."

Doc and I have met again -- quite a few times in New York City when I was teaching at Yale for a year and he was doctoring in Queens, and then in Nashville, then in New Hampshire where he still works, and once at a Third Platoon reunion. At some point in each of these visits, we feel the old anger well up as we re-tell the Pace story.

And I ask myself the question: did Pace get what he wanted from the war? I'm positive he makes sure that people know he received a medal given for valor. Did he stay in the Army for 20 years, trading on his medal? Or does the memory of his close call, and his subsequent cowardliness, percolate through his memories and sour his constructed story of Pace as hero?

Chapter Eight

Don't Mean Nothin'

These talks with Doc also sparked in me an assessment of my war. I pondered the usual: the randomness of who lived and who died, the pain loved ones back home felt as their young sons died or, in my case, as they received frightening telegrams, and the survivor's guilt that has weighed on so many of my old platoon buddies (and my cousin as well, who is alive because of a last-minute replacement for him on a mission up by the DMZ).

But I also asked, what did I get out of it? I made it home, back to a safer and saner place, where I was able (after only one divorce) to have a deeply fulfilling marriage and family life, enjoy friends, go to football games, and enjoy the small and large daily pleasures of life. Back in the rice paddies and jungles, this had been my goal. And to be sure, I had had a rare experience, one that many people recognize as such. (*You were in Vietnam? You were shot? I've never known someone who was in combat! Did you kill anybody?*) But it didn't give me some unique insight into the meaning of life, and it surely didn't give me a mysterious, haunted visage that attracted women.

There have been some positive consequences, I began to realize. When events seem like crises to those around me, I put them in perspective by asking, is someone going to die? And I remember how intimate my squad was, despite our having come from such different places. It taught me that at bottom, your love for people comes from some deep shared humanity, not from how much money you each have, or whether you are black or white, or whether you enjoy Proust instead of tractor pulls.

And I began to realize that my war will never be over. Over the years, I could usually talk easily about the events themselves in the war: the firefights, the wounds, the hardships. This, to me, didn't mean the war was still with me. I still believed I was basically unaffected, that telling the war stories was like telling about a baseball game in which I had played.

But I couldn't talk about how I had felt during those events. I didn't know myself -- or perhaps I didn't want to admit to myself -- how frightened I had been. Occasionally I would feel a welling-up as memories flitted through my mind or as I was describing an event, but I felt foolish about it, embarrassed. After all, I hadn't had it so bad: no hot LZ, no human wave attacks, just small dirty firefights and booby traps. Crying about my little war, I thought, was just being "full of tears and flapdoodle."

We had had a catchall phrase in Vietnam: "Don't mean nothin'." It helped us smooth over the reality of our unnatural life. Dead people? Don't mean nothin'. A queasy hard-to-describe feeling after trying to kill other human beings, while other human beings try to kill you? Don't mean nothin'. Somebody killed? Don't mean nothin'. Feel ashamed because you were glad you weren't hit instead of your friend? Don't mean nothin'.

Looking back, I realize that, however small my war was, it wasn't natural, at least for most of us. Whatever hard-to-articulate feelings I'd had, I had buried them deep inside. How else were we to have coped? There was no time (and no inclination by the army back then) to interrupt the war and take us somewhere safe where we could talk with therapists. Dwelling on what had happened the day before could leave you not paying attention to what was happening today, and that could be fatal.

The war is also still with Doc, and with those that remain from our old platoon. I know because we had a reunion in 2007. About a dozen of us met in Pigeon Forge, Tennessee. Most of us had not seen each other since 1969. Jerry Morehouse and Dan Weirich, though, had kept in touch, much like Doc and myself, ever since Vietnam. Jerry had been the force behind the reunion, having used the internet to locate many of us.

Not all the survivors came. Ferrell, who had been patched up by Doc when he walked point into the NVA base camp, said he was just not ready to deal with Vietnam in as intense a setting as a reunion. Alan Schmitt, who was paralyzed and in a wheelchair, said his psychiatrist told him he was not ready either. Jesse Rabenda had changed his name and refused to talk to Jerry or Dan. He eventually answered my email, and told me he was a Chicago cop. We agreed to try and get together sometime. But he would not come to the reunion. Lloyd Cook, Jerry found out, had been in and out of jail since Vietnam, and was "in" at the moment. Gallion would not answer his phone himself and had instructed his wife to not let us talk with him. Lewis also declined: his brother, who also had been in our company, indicated that Larry didn't talk about the war.

We didn't invite Pace.

Rashomon-like, we talked about our experiences. But unlike in the movie, we did reach some consensus on most of what had happened. Jerry had a collection of pictures he had taken (I never took any, and wondered how he and others had kept cameras working in the humidity of Vietnam). He had a picture of the massed burned, dead NVA on the hillside outside of the Brigade Main Base in Long Binh I had passed on the way to the field. All of us had called them the "crispy critters" when we had talked about them back then, and we still did as we looked at the photo. He had a picture of the medic who preceded Doc sticking his knee in the wounded side of a VC, getting him to tell where he had thrown the bundle of rifles he had tossed away as the platoon closed on him. And Reid Mendehall had pictures of dozens of dead NVA, hung up in concertina wire, who had died in the human wave attacks in Cambodia.

We looked at these pictures (which I would discover unsettled non-veterans like my wife), and re-hashed our fights and our disdain for Pace, again and again. It was, I think, our way of coming to grips with the experience. Our conversations reminded me of the old joke:

"How many combat veterans does it take to change a lightbulb?" Answer: "You'll never know. You had to be there."

And for me, I found out what had happened to the others, in Vietnam and in later life.

For years, every time I visited Los Angeles, I had looked in the phone book for a Richard Dixon, and had never found one. So when I first visited the Vietnam Memorial Wall, I was nervous, my heart pumping hard, as I looked through the list of names, afraid I would find him there. He wasn't listed, though, and I held out hope I would one day see him again. But though he wasn't on the Memorial, the war had indeed claimed him. After over a year in Letterman Army Hospital in San Francisco, he lost his leg. Some years later, he died in a motorcycle accident: he had rigged up a way to ride with only one foot, and the mechanism had failed and put him in front of an oncoming car.

Jackson, I was told, had returned to the squad the day after I had been shot, and the next day had been shot in his neck. No one had been able to locate him for the reunion, though.

And four days after I had been shot, James Clarkson, only son, had been killed in an ambush. Our reunion was in part being held to coincide with a memorial service for him in his nearby town in northwest Georgia.

Jerry, Dan Weirich, Curtiss Dewitt, Bill Preston, Rick Laub, and Reid Mendenhall all had suffered from some degree of post-traumatic stress disorder. Jerry cannot sleep unless he is sitting up, alert and ready to react at a moment's notice. Dan, a college graduate when he was drafted, had never been able to shake the memories, and lives what I would call a reclusive life in a cabin by a lake outside of Knoxville, Tennessee. Curtis continually dreams of waking up in a casket. Reid had survived a human-wave attack at a firebase in Cambodia, and was one of the first PTSD diagnoses.

Bill Preston ended up serving thirty years in the army, ending as a Sergeant-Major. When he had gone back to the rear to re-enlist during the time Pace cut his leg, he had marched into headquarters straight from the field, muddy and unshaven. As he tells it, they asked him in what MOS he wanted to reenlist. He looked at their shiny boots, their crisp, starched uniforms, and their air-conditioned office, and told them, "Whatever MOS you guys are in." So he went into Administration. He, like Jerry, had not been with their squad when four of the six sent out had died in an ambush. Eventually, the survivor guilt came back and haunted him.

Sergeant Unger, I learned, had been haunted for years by the death of Green, a fellow squad member who had drowned while crossing a river, in line between Unger and Jerry. He had gone under the surface and been swept down by the current. His body was never recovered. Jerry and Dave Unger had anguished over the years about whether they had tried hard enough to catch him.

I felt lucky. I occasionally have a dream in which an NVA is crawling around the edge of an APC, and I don't have my rifle, so jump on top of him, crushing his AK to his chest so he cannot shoot me. My wife then wakes me up, pinned underneath me as she tries to breath. But most of the time, my life has not been hamstrung by memories or bad dreams.

And my luck still holds. At 65 years old I had a stroke, but a small one from which I recovered fully within two hours. The doctors assured me I had been very lucky: the clot must have been very small to have dissolved so quickly. The neurologists could not find a reason for the stroke: my heart and arteries were "pristine," they said.

But two years earlier I had seen a vascular surgeon about my left arm: the circulation had greatly diminished. At that time he investigated and told me the vein that connected the carotid to my arm had failed. Nothing could be done. It meant my arm was weaker and colder, but I still had use of it.

The vascular surgeon had been alerted about my stroke, because the arm problem was in my records. He looked at the scans of my neck and chest, and deduced that the site of the old graft was probably ulcerated, and had created a pocket where blood swirled and formed clots. Days after the stroke, he removed the bad vein graft, finding numerous blood clots at the ulcerated spot.

My stroke had been caused by a small clot instead of one of the big ones the surgeon discovered. And they had discovered the cause of the stroke, and removed it. Again, I felt lucky.

All of this caused the old war memories to again become vivid. I now realize that they will always resurface at some point. But I found that, like the reunion pictures of what we experienced, they didn't bother me. I know I will never understand the unfocused emotional state I sometimes feel when remembering the war. But the memories are just memories: Vietnam was a big part, but does not have to be the most important part, of my life.

And on October 17th of every year, the anniversary of the day I got drafted, I celebrate another anniversary instead: the birth of my oldest son.

-END-

Made in the USA
San Bernardino, CA
30 April 2018